I0698478

"David Risselada is a fresh new voice in conservative publications. He has written a thought-provoking book which should be read by all Americans who are concerned about the direction our country is taking."

David L. Goetsch,
author of *Liberal Tyranny in Higher Education*

"David has been contributing insightful material to Sons of Liberty Media for more than five years. He has great insight into the brainwashing methods used by the left to implement their agenda and can articulate it well."

Tim Brown, Editor, Writer,
Sons of Liberty Media

Without a Shot Indeed

Inducing Compliance to Tyranny Through Conditioning and Persuasion

David Risselada

www.TotalPublishingAndMedia.com

Copyright © 2021, David Risselada

All rights reserved.
No part of this book may be reproduced, stored in a retrieval system,
or transmitted by any means, electronic, mechanical, photocopying,
recording, or otherwise, without written permission from the author.

ISBN 978-1-63302-191-4

Table of Contents

Acknowledgements

I would like to thank my wife Deborah, for her patience and hours spent listening to each chapter as I read it to her over and over. My professors at Liberty University for showing me every college is not a lost cause. Tim Brown, Bradlee Dean, David Goetsch and Fred Deruvo for supporting my writing, and everyone else who told me to get my butt up and keep going when I was ready to sit down a while.

Forward

This book will examine the psychological methods employed by the political left to change America from a free republic to a socialist dictatorship. The material presented is the culmination of a decade of study, motivated by an understanding the communists have developed a sophisticated knowledge of human behavior.

Soviet Premier Nikita Khrushchev proudly proclaimed the U.S. would fall without a shot being fired because of the gullibility of the American citizen. He was able to say this because the communists had mastered the arts of behavioral manipulation and persuasion.

The average American remains blissfully unaware of the methodologies being employed against them through the media, the education system and other major institutions. They do not know the extent to which our behaviors, reactions and attitudes are studied for the purpose of formulating strategies and planning agendas.

Through the examination of psychological theories like operant conditioning, education techniques like critical theory and how a science of human behavior was developed through the theory of evolution; this book will examine the conditioning processes that have brought us to the point where people are willingly complying with tyrannical dictates.

If there is one thing to take away from this book it is the knowledge that man is viewed through the lens of a godless science, and it is believed our thoughts and behaviors can be guided and shaped to accept the communist agenda. These conclusions are reached based on simple observations of how we react to the stimuli they feed us. By the end of the book the reader will have a firm understanding of what the powers that be understand about human behavior and how to manipulate it to their ends.

Americans are marching to the drumbeat of their own enslavement when it comes to Covid-19 and the enforced wearing of facemasks. The chapters in this book go through the steps of how our behaviors were manipulated and our thoughts controlled, to the point where most of us willingly comply with tyranny. Most people are not even stopping to ask themselves why they are being forced to wear a mask, or distance themselves from loved ones. They simply comply because they do not know what else to do. They are simply responding to a stimulus, fed to them by people seeking to change their behaviors.

This book was originally accepted by Liberty Hill publishers at the end of December 2020. Towards the end of January, they sent me the first initial review and recommended edits where they said the following –

> "Through a powerful look at the changes taking place in the culture and society of the United

States, the author takes readers on a journey to discovering the truth behind these changes and how political agenda is leading to the termination of American freedoms. With excellent insight and applicable teaching, *Without a Shot Indeed: Inducing Compliance to Tyranny* encourages readers to open their eyes to the reality of America in the postmodern age, inspiring Americans to fight for the preservation of their freedoms." (Liberty Hill Publishers)

I was thrilled, of course, and feeling good about the project. After making the recommended edits, however, they contacted me and said it would be inappropriate for them to publish it because of its controversial nature. For a moment, I prided myself for having a book that was deemed too controversial. How funny.

Introduction
Understanding Change

I awoke this morning to a dream so strange.
I dreamt the world was different, it somehow had changed.
Just how glorious can this beautiful world be?
You must start by being, the change you wish to see.

C hange. It is something the whole world longs for yet, very few take any action to affect. In recent years, our country has been going through major changes. Mostly driven by the hard-political left who, for some reason, view our nation as illegitimate and in need of a makeover. They have all but admitted their end goal is the transformation of America as a beacon of liberty and individualism, to just another collectivist nation in a global governing body.

People on the left believe collectivism represents a Utopian paradise where the government can guarantee the equality of outcomes; and wealth, (in some type of fairytale fashion) is evenly distributed across the board. It does not matter how many times you show them the historical failures of collectivist societies; they remain convinced America needs to change. They are committed to action and willing to do anything to achieve their goal.

The political right, on the other hand, has largely sat back believing the type of change the left seeks will never happen. They believe the constitution protects our individual rights, therefore, action on our part is not needed. Conservatives love America and, for the most part, believe success can be found in the individual pursuit of happiness. Where they have failed is not realizing the lengths their political opponents are willing to go to bring about the change they wish to see.

The worldviews which govern the political philosophies of conservatives and liberals are vastly different. So different in fact, the right has a hard time understanding the left's approach because it is so alien to conservative thinking. Being mostly Christian, the American right is governed by a universal morality which dictates the way we view right and wrong.

Leftists who seek to transform our nation have adopted an "ends justify the means" mentality towards change. They do not share in the Christian worldview and tend to cling to a Darwinian explanation of mankind's origins. Darwin, of course, founded the theory of evolution, which has become the basis of scientific education in America. Christianity and Darwinism are two distinctly different cultural perspectives which are not compatible. Darwin believed human beings have no soul and were just another animal whose existence was without significant meaning. There is no universal morality defining right and wrong or what is acceptable behavior. This is the basis of the ends justifying the means mentality.

Operating from this perspective, the hard left has adopted an Alinsky-type mentality towards change. Saul Alinsky's Rules for Radicals has become universally known as the playbook for the Democrat party, yet it remains largely misunderstood. Worse yet, many on the right refuse to believe people could sink to such depths, or conduct themselves in such a deprived manner. Alinsky taught that people in pursuit of change should not concern themselves with the approach they take, only the ends they seek. Ethics and morality are not something Alinsky concerned himself with.

To the left, morality on a universal scale does not exist. There is no principle defining a universal right or wrong when it comes to social change. If it is achievable, and it works, it is right. Alinsky explains that true morality is a willingness to corrupt yourself in pursuit of the greater good. Those who care more about personal salvation, he argued, were not willing to sacrifice their own sense of morality for what was best for the people; therefore, they did not care about society, only themselves. No morality from this perspective is in a roundabout way, a higher level of morality. Furthermore, he argued that corruption is a social construct of sorts that also does not exist. If morality is nonexistent on a universal level, how can the concept of corruption exist? One cannot exist without the other. Corrupted means, he argued, do not corrupt the ends. This approach towards change explains a great deal in the types of things we have witnessed in the recent past.

To Alinsky, the right would be considered means and ends moralists. This means that the political right places limits on what they are willing to do based on Christian morality. Believing in personal salvation, conservatives are not willing to corrupt themselves in pursuit of change, while the left is willing to do whatever it takes with no regard to the consequences. Alinsky argued that means and ends moralists always find themselves on the losing end of any battle because of their own self constraints. While liberals are willing to be deceitful, conservative Christians, for the most part, are not. Alinsky describes the Jews from WWII Germany as being means and ends moralists. From his view, it was their religious underpinnings that kept them from doing what was necessary to save themselves.

The problem for the left is truth and universal morality do exist. It is wrong no matter what way you look at it, to lie, cheat, and steal your way to victory. To argue corrupted means will not corrupt the ends is to suggest that man is the ultimate decider of what constitutes morality, leaving God's word with no meaning. There is simply no way pushing an agenda based on lies, deceit, and corruption will result in the great Utopia they believe it will. The only possibility arising from such depraved methods is a corrupted world devoid of absolute truth. Freedom cannot exist in such a world.

Of course, the quest for societal change in America goes back further than Alinsky. The left has been professionally organizing for decades with the goal of turning America into a socialist nation. Former Soviet Premier Nikita Khrushchev said that America would be transformed one step at a time into a communist country by feeding us small doses of socialism. He said Americans were gullible, and that through this approach, they would take America without firing a shot. This approach is known as Fabianism.

Fabian Socialism came about out of a desire to avoid the revolutionary approach of the Marxists. Fabianism's primary approach was to implement socialism in an incremental fashion through democratic methods as opposed to force. In other words, socialism in America would be achieved through voting. This is an approach that has been largely successful. With the federal government being firmly in control of education, it can be argued that children are being trained to believe in, support, and eventually vote for socialist policies.

We see this playing out every day. The left has infiltrated our schools and taught our kids the values and traditions we grew up with are essentially wrong. They are being trained to be gun control and climate change activists, they are taught the nation is founded on racist principles, to view biological gender as a social construct, and finally, to view America in general as an oppressive nation based on greed. In other words, they are being trained in Marxist ideology and until recently, this went largely unnoticed.

Fabianism and the Alinsky approach are intertwined in a sense because Alinsky based much of what he wrote on Fabian principles. To get people to willingly vote for socialist policies, they must first be given a choice. Socialism must appeal to their senses. It must be compared to something else while being presented as a superior method of governing. The competing choice must be presented as a system which is responsible for nothing but suffering. This is what is occurring in our public schools. Americanism, liberty, and individualism are all being characterized as a vehicle of oppression while socialism is being presented as a superior system that will ultimately save us. Alinsky said that people can be brought to accept the change they may not otherwise if, their future appears to be hopeless. By presenting America as an oppressive, racist nation they are training our children to advocate for change. The change they are being trained to view favorably is socialism. In essence, they are being trained to become the change the left wants them to be.

Another way of explaining this process is commonly known as the problem-reaction-solution strategy, otherwise known as the Hegelian Dialectic. Georg Hegel's theory on dialectical materialism was adopted by Karl Marx to back up his theory of economic communism. Dialectical materialism is a theory which posits the idea that all change is accomplished through struggle. When applied at a societal level this dialectical process works to keep us trapped in a certain way of thinking. The media assists in this process by creating panic and defining the narrative that keeps our attention and gets us talking. If the public stays focused on the media's dangling carrot and argues within the parameters defined by them, the public consciousness is easily guided into a predetermined solution benefiting the government. This is also the way it works in the classroom. Public issues and policies are discussed with the intent of persuading students to see a need for change.

How do I know all of this? What motivated me for example, to study Alinsky, Fabianism or, the Hegelian Dialectic? I witnessed all of this as a student at Northeastern State University in Broken Arrow Oklahoma. I was a student in their social work program which was dominated by progressives who believe America needs to be brought down and reformed. Everything about this nation was racist, homophobic, sexist, and imperialistic.

At the time, I was in my late 30's and was not nearly as politically aware as I am today. I did notice, however, that many of the students in the program had a pre-existing belief which aligned with the instructors. They hated this country and were arguing for social change. Amazingly, many of these students had no idea what it was they were advocating for. For example, one student would always accentuate the words "social change" in his arguments. I had asked what it was specifically about America he wanted to fix and if he understood the significance of the bill of rights. He replied by saying he did not care about the constitution and only wanted free health care. Sadly, this was the mentality of most of the students in the program. They had already been properly conditioned through elementary education to have the politically correct worldview.

Health care is an issue that was presented using the techniques described in this chapter. In the textbook we were using there was a simple comparison made. The book presented America's health care system as broken and inaccessible to most people. Health care in socialist countries, however, is free. That was it. The rest of the chapter was dedicated to problems with the American medical system while only making one comment about socialized medicine. It is free. This is referred to as an application of critical theory. Students are encouraged to criticize their own country and culture. The textbook, from the student's perspective, carries the weight of officialdom. So, it must be true.

Race and white privilege were also big issues. During a research and statistics class, I had a professor suggest that it was acceptable to "nudge" the results of a study if it did not meet the results you were expecting. He was speaking specifically about racism. Social work depends on marginalized populations needing social services. To them, being a minority meant you were automatically marginalized. There was this mentality suggesting minorities were to be treated as oppressed victims in a white hegemonic system. This is the basis for Critical Race Theory. Everything about our society is racist and white people, knowingly or not, harbor an unconscious bias towards minorities. Changing the results of a study then, in his mind, is justified because people do not how racist they are.

My first self-published book, *Not on My Watch: Exposing the Marxist Agenda in Education* was an attempt to share my experiences at Northeastern State and what I learned about social change and the left-wing agenda. I was told that I was not fit for the profession because of my opposition to concepts like social justice and white privilege.

My professor literally told me that she was the gate keeper, and her job was to ensure that all people coming into the field were ideologically aligned. This is because the field depends on the redistribution of wealth to function. If you are an individual who believes in limited government, personal responsibility, and that taxation is theft, you are not aligned with social work objectives.

I was not the only individual to experience such a thing. The National Association of Scholars published an article entitled *The Scandal of Social Work Education*[1] highlighting the political motives of the profession and their attempts to indoctrinate people into leftist thinking. One story tells of a student who endured the same scrutinization as me while working as an intern at a state representative's office. He wrote a conservative welfare reform proposal and was denied his degree.

What I witnessed in this program was so appalling, so disturbing, that I became obsessed with researching what was going on. I saw the connections between what was happening in the college and the events that were taking place in the real world. For example, The occupy Wall Street Protests were occurring at the time. They were professionally organized attempts to discredit capitalism and promote socialism. Organizers were showing up to the college in an attempt to recruit students into the movement.

I also watched in absolute amazement as students one by one, stood in front of the class and admitted they had no idea how racist they were until being taught about their white privilege. I realized that education was being used to train students to accept socialism and literally view America as a problem that prevents the world from coming together under one big happy banner. I wanted everyone to be aware so, I began writing about it.

I realized if things were going to get better, if our country was to survive, it would take a massive awakening of the people. Freedom can only exist if the population is informed and actively paying attention to what is happening around them. Sadly, this is not the case in America. Most people, and understandably so, (I am not trying to belittle anyone here) have lived under the belief that we are free, and that our liberties are constitutionally protected for so long, that believing we could lose them to socialism is a pill that is hard to swallow. Any attempts to draw attention to the correlations between what is happening in America and how socialism has been implemented in the past will likely leave one labeled a conspiracy theorist.

The bigger point is that if we expect our children or grandchildren to live in the same free country we grew up in, we must know what is going on and, we must know how to articulate the right arguments. We must educate ourselves and be the change *we* wish to see. Kleon Skousen said in *The Naked Communist*[2] if enough people would study and come to understand the problem we face; we could see freedom for all men in our lifetime. Unfortunately, he said this in 1958.

The left sees America as a nation in need of a makeover. They have committed themselves to changing the very ideological underpinnings which have kept us going since our founding. They, in essence, have become the change they want to see and have consistently demonstrated that there is nothing they are not willing to do to get what they want.

Chapter One
Framing the Problem

The argument that the two parties should represent opposed ideals and policies... is a foolish idea. Instead, the two parties should be almost identical, so that the American people can throw the rascals out at any election without leading to any profound or extensive shifts in policy. Then it should be possible to replace it, every four years if necessary, by the other party which will be none of these things but will still pursue, with new vigor, approximately the same basic policies. (Quigley, *Tragedy and Hope: A History of the World in Our Time*)

America certainly has changed. While many believe the Presidency of Barack Obama is primarily responsible for many of the sweeping changes we have witnessed, the truth is a little more complicated.

President Obama, no doubt, brought the issue of change to the forefront of the American consciousness. It could be theoretically argued this was the culmination of a decades-long process and not the beginning. Barack Obama was a skilled orator who tapped into the deeper feelings of discontent felt by so many Americans, both on the left and the right. For eight years prior to Obama,

America has been bogged down in endless wars and deficit spending. The common perception of the Bush administration among the left was that he was a big corporate crony who had no concern for the little man. By the end of his eight years in office, George Bush had increased the national debt (in the same manner that every other president seems to do by the way) by over four trillion dollars.[3]

At the end of Bush's eight years, Americans had enough and were ready for change. You could argue they had been brought to a state of hopelessness, if you will, and were looking for a charismatic leader to take the country in a new direction. Barack Obama was an individual many people did not understand, but they were willing to give his vision a try because they were fed up with the mess the Bush administration had created. For all his promises and skillfully delivered rhetoric, Obama later proved to be the same as the old boss in terms of spending and war. In his first three years in office, he had increased the national debt more than Bush in his entire eight years.[4] Obama also increased Bush's wars in the middle east after insisting he would end them. By the end of 2009, he had carried out more unmanned drone strikes than Bush had throughout his entire tenure as a wartime president by bombing seven countries, and, getting us involved in two additional wars without congressional approval.[5]

A person's first impression when examining these facts is that there is no difference between the Bush and Obama administrations. Ironically, when it comes to the wars in the Middle East, both Bush and Obama were carrying out the same objectives laid out in a document which outlined the strategy for maintaining American military dominance. This document was called *Rebuilding America's Defenses,*[6] otherwise known as The Project New American Century. In March 2007, a video surfaced of General Wesley Clark[7] explaining how he discovered the Bush administration's plans to not only invade Iraq but Syria, Lebanon, Libya, Somalia, Sudan, and eventually Iran.

During his presidency, Obama not only managed to bomb three of the countries on this list, Libya, Somalia, and Syria but Pakistan and Yemen as well.[8] It is important to note that the Project New American Century document was written in 1997, during the Clinton administration. America's initial involvement in Somalia was under Clinton's watch and, according to Alternet.com,[9] Clinton expanded the crippling sanctions against an already devastated Iraq. Which of course, was suffering due to the first Iraq war launched by George Bush senior in 1991.

Are you starting to see a pattern? Barack Obama carried out the war plans initiated by George Bush under plans written in 1997 which built on the actions taken by George Bush senior in 1991. What this essentially equates to is Republicans and Democrats pretending to hate each other but carrying out the same major policy initiatives, while keeping us distracted with their circus sideshows. More on that later.

The unfortunate reality with these Middle Eastern wars is that they have nothing to do with securing our freedom or way of life. Iraq posed no military threat to the United States any more than any of these other countries did. We invaded Iraq because Saddam Hussein was threatening to sell oil in Euros, and not U.S. Dollars. This would have devastated the U.S. economy. The same is True with Libya as well. In fact, our entire economic might is based on the premise that Saudi Arabia props up our money by enforcing oil sales in U.S. dollars in exchange for U.S. military muscle.[10]

Whether people want to believe it or not, Donald Trump has carried out the same agenda. Not only has the Trump administration increased the number of drone strikes being conducted, which incidentally is leading to a higher number of civilian casualties, but he has also relaxed the rules which govern such actions.[11] According to The American Conservative website, Trump has quadrupled the number of airstrikes against Somalia.

Not only is President Trump carrying out the same war agenda as his predecessors, but he is also increasing the national debt. In fact, in his first three years as president he increased the debt more than Obama did during his whole presidency. A whopping 5.2 trillion dollars to be exact.[12]

The larger point being made is that people put a lot of hope in a politician's promises only to see there are no profound differences in the policies they pursue. Carroll Quigley, author of the book *Tragedy and Hope: A History of the World in our Time,*[13] alluded to this idea by pointing out our two-party political system is one where Democrats and Republicans pretend to oppose one another. On issues of non-importance, they fight like cats and dogs, but behind the scenes, they work together to advance a globalist agenda. Many people would brush this off as a conspiracy theory, however, it bears a certain truth when our government is closely examined.

The public has been conditioned to accept without question, their chosen party's policy initiatives. A mentality has taken over the mind to the point where words like "never Trumper" are used for conservatives who are questioning anything Trump does. When Obama was president, any skepticism towards his policy initiatives equated to racism. These are tactics used to silence opposition and distract us from the truth. While we are bickering over such nonsense, the facts remain that President Trump, Obama and Bush have all carried out the same agenda of huge deficit spending and war.

There are more examples. It is difficult to believe that the Democrats hate Donald Trump as much as they pretend to. He not only signed off on all the spending bills sent to him, he also set the stage for further gun control with his actions on bump stocks and support for red flag laws. After the Parkland school shooting in 2018, Donald Trump sat right next to Dianne Feinstein, a known hater of the second amendment, and suggested on live television that firearms should be confiscated before an individual deemed to be a danger to himself or others is afforded due process.[14]

This is just another example of how the Democrats and Republicans are working together to advance an agenda while pretending to be diametrically opposed to one another. Red flag laws and the bump stock ban, which illegally redefined the term machine gun,[15] literally destroy the second amendment while setting the stage for gun confiscation. The bump stock ban could potentially destroy the concept of the grandfather clause.

What America is really witnessing is a change strategy, an ongoing effort to keep people invested in the two-party system. Every four years it is the same story. We must vote for whichever candidate our chosen party is pushing to save the country. For Republicans, it is Donald Trump. The same holds true for Democrats, they believe Trump is a fascist, racist, capitalist pig and only Joe Biden can save the nation. This is ridiculous, as it has been demonstrated that the two parties are pursuing the same agendas.

Saul Alinsky wrote in *Rules for Radicals*[16] that people can be brought into accepting the change they may not otherwise if they are in a state of hopelessness, or if they have no faith in the prevailing system. He says people are willing to embrace an unknown future if they have no hope in the current situation. This is essentially what is occurring every four years. People grow tired of the same old lies and dirty politics they put all their hopes in the individual who knows how to pander to their beliefs. This is how they incrementally shift the attitude of the country in their favor and get people to accept change they may have not otherwise and, behave in ways they generally would not. It could be theoretically argued that they are using the sciences of persuasion to push the country in the direction they want it to go.

There is reason to speculate that the sciences of human behavior are being used to persuade or push the attitudes of the masses in certain directions. In the book *The Dynamics of Persuasion: Communication and attitudes in the 21st century,* Richard Perloff discusses the technique of *fear then relief.* [17] This is described as the persuader intentionally placing the intended target into a state of fear, then replacing it with a less frightening alternative.

According to Perloff, this technique is effective because the sense of relief experienced when the fear is replaced is overwhelming and reinforcing. The sensation is associated with the following request for compliance. A good example would be the acceptance of Donald Trump's bump stock ban. There was much fear and anticipation over what types of gun bans might be implemented after the Las Vegas shooting, people were relieved the only action taken was the ban on a firearm accessory.

Perloff notes that the association between relief and the following request for compliance can be so powerful, people are often in a state of mindlessness and less attentive than normal. When it came to this seemingly useless piece of plastic, for instance, people completely ignored how the

ATF illegally redefined the term machine gun in the existing gun control laws to include devices like bump stocks.

This technique could, in theory, be applied to elections in general. In America, the term *the lesser of two evils* is a commonly accepted theme used to explain the acceptance of a candidate who may not live up to our expectations. This is the fear then relief principle put into action. The election of Barack Obama for example, was a sure win because people had become so weary and hopeless during the Bush years that they were, like Alinsky said, willing to accept the change they did not fully understand. The same could be applied in the 2016 election of Donald Trump as well. People were so overwhelmingly relieved that Hillary Clinton did not win that they have, as Perloff noted, become more susceptible to persuasive techniques and less attentive to what Donald Trump is doing, opposed to what he says.

To avoid the impression of singling out Donald Trump, the technique worked the same with Obama. Liberal Democrats were so elated with the sensation of relief they questioned nothing the man did because in their minds, they averted the disaster of another Republican winning the presidency.

The effectiveness of the fear then relief strategy depends on how well the initial fear appeal is crafted. A message designed to invoke fear is done to scare people into changing their positions by showing the negative consequences for failing to do so.[18]

Political campaigns are without a doubt structured around the idea that voting for the other guy will lead to wanton destruction. Republicans and Democrats alike, effectively play on the fears of their voters, targeting the known values of their demographic. Democrats know their voters are afraid of Republicans cutting welfare programs for the poor, so they craft their message specifically invoking that fear by characterizing Republicans as selfish corporatists who only care about profit. Republicans do the same, capitalizing on Democrats' attempts to pass gun control. Republicans talk a big game but do little of anything with substance when it comes to defending liberty.

Fear messages can be effective, but unfortunately for the people crafting them, they are not always. If for example, the issue does not resonate with the target audience the message will fall on deaf ears. People who are not into politics for example, are not generally persuaded by political campaigns and the messages revolving around them have little effect in swaying opinion. People who are rooted in their convictions are also less likely to be affected by fear messages.

Interestingly, there is some evidence suggesting persuaders are intentionally targeting what they refer to as, mindless people. For example, in an article entitled *Fear-then-Relief: Mindlessness and cognitive deficits,*[19] the authors make the claim that people, when experiencing the relief of realizing the fear stimulus was unfounded, fall into a mindless, reactionary mode for a brief time where the arousal of the relief sensation makes them more susceptible to persuasive communications. Studies have shown, according to this article, when people experience the relief sensation, they are less likely to ask any questions pertaining to the following requests for compliance. According to the authors, this suggests that a state of mindlessness is produced with the relief, making one more likely to simply go along with whatever requests may follow.

If there is any truth to Quigley's assertion about the two political parties working together, then it can be assumed they are also working to deliver a carefully constructed message designed to keep you in the dark. Political speeches are designed to invoke fear over social issues and motivate people to join social movements.[20] They are almost always used in the pursuit of hidden goals and political objectives designed to persuade voters in one direction or another. Research shows that when politicians frame their political messages in terms of their voter's values, opposed to their own, they are more likely to get them to change their positions[21]. Understanding the attitudes, beliefs, and concerns of the target audience is crucial when it comes to developing a message intended to change someone's opinion.

For example, in an article appearing in The New York Times in 2015 entitled The *Key to Political Persuasion,*[22] Willer and Feinberg argue that to persuade opinion change among people holding opposite values, you must get inside their heads, understand the values they hold, and reframe the positions you are arguing in terms of those values. Liberal politicians could theoretically convince conservative voters to change their attitudes on certain positions by framing their argument in terms of the values conservatives associate themselves with. According to Willer and Feinberg, when social issues like same sex-marriage are presented in a way reflecting what conservative voters hold dear; freedom, liberty, and patriotism, they are more likely to support it. This technique is known as framing.

Framing of a political message is studied in all areas of human behavior and is depicted by the way a media source, or a politician, presents a social issue to motivate action in resolving it[23]. Framing, according to Nelson, Zoe & Rosalee (1997) is psychologically effective because it shapes how the public perceives certain issues. For instance, the political left has been successful in framing their messages concerning gun violence and targeting the people that are most likely to be motivated by it. Furthermore, by targeting people of a more conservative-leaning, who view gun ownership in terms of hunting and collecting, opposed to self-defense and the preservation of a free state, they have been able to sway many opinions against ownership of the popular Ar-15 rifle.

A good example is an article by Daniel Hayes entitled *I am an AR-15 owner and I have had enough.*[24] This article is intended to persuade opinion change by framing the argument against AR-15 ownership from the perspective of someone who owns one and is starting to view it in a different light due to the recent rash of mass shootings. It is an effective article in terms of defining the conservative argument for gun ownership but contrasting it with the liberal argument about how dangerous AR-15 rifles allegedly are. This is the same kind of technique Barack Obama employed when he claimed his views on homosexual marriage evolved. When running for president, he took a solid stand against the issue but later changed his position. He did this from the perspective that he had gained a morally superior position with the intention of gaining support from a population that largely opposed it.

Research indicates that people will view framed messages from the view of their own personal biases.[25] For example, if the article concerning AR-15 rifles was meant to persuade opinion change, then the focus is to put emphasis on the negative aspects of the rifles while targeting the most likely demographic that will be affected by the message. Those gun owners who do not own them and view gun ownership strictly from a hunting or collecting perspective.

Framing is also done by presenting the same information in different ways. For example, a doctor suggesting you have a 4 out of 5 chance of surviving surgery, or a 1 out of 5 chance of dying from it. Both scenarios present the same information but are framed differently. According to Cass Sunstein, who was the head of the White House office of information and regulatory affairs under Barack Obama, framing works to influence opinion because people lack the necessary cognitive skill needed to double-check to see how their opinion may change if the problem was presented differently.[26] He also claims people would not know what to do about the contradiction between what they thought they believed and the choice they are making based on the way the argument is framed. He is essentially saying that people are too gullible to know their choices and opinions are being manipulated.

Referencing the AR-15 article once again, it could be theorized that the people targeted for that message would default to the position that taking a stand against AR-15 rifles would create a safer society. Everybody, regardless of their position of the second amendment, wants to see an end to mass shootings. By framing this article in a manner which presents an AR-15 owner going through a moral dilemma, it is hoped that other people will change their opinion as well.

According to Perloff,[27] social scientists and philosophers have theorized for years about the best methods to craft a message to influence attitude and or, opinion change. Returning to the previous section's discussion on fear messages, a well-framed argument will contain the element of fear but also a recommended course of action to alleviate that fear, or avert the potential danger causing it. Perloff states that "a fear-arousing message contains two basic elements: threat and efficacy information, or a problem and a solution. A message must first threaten the individual, convincing him or her that dangers lurk in the environment."[28]

The American media is infamous for presenting the news in a manner that suggests there is always a danger, and freedom itself is a dangerous concept. There is always a problem and a potential solution. This solution generally leads to less freedom for the individual and more control for the government.

This method of framing arguments bears a striking similarity to something called the Hegelian Dialectic. This is based on dialectical materialism,[29] which according to Ray Nunes, who was once chair of the Worker's Party in the 1990s', is central to the Marxist push for social change.

Dialectical materialism posits the idea all progress is made through conflict, and because matter existed before conscious thought, progress through conflicting matter has brought us to where we are. The Hegelian Dialectic[30] is based on the ideas of Georg Hegel and applied to Frederick Engels and Karl Marx's theories on communism. It is also known as the problem-reaction-solution strategy. The idea is to strike fear into the hearts of the masses, which would motivate them to demand change and implement the solution, which has already been predetermined.

There are numerous examples to draw from. Anytime the media is pushing a fear message or framing an argument, it is being done with the intent of influencing opinion or attitude change and/or motivating the masses into an action of some kind. The left's argument to completely defund the police is a good example. This argument forces the right to take the opposite position, even though there are several well-reasoned arguments in the middle as to why some police reforms may be needed. No knock raids and asset forfeiture are good examples. The argument is now framed from the perspective of either defunding the police completely or showing one hundred percent support for everything they do. This is a brilliant strategy if the end goal is to grow the state's police powers.

Another example is the 2020 presidential election. How would you get the public to demand a national identification card, or question the electoral college or even accept an increase in government power in general? Present the masses with a broken down, corrupted, unworkable election system and force them to demand change.

Finally, and this will be discussed again later, the Covid-19 scare of 2020. The media, along with the government at the national and international levels, played a brilliant game of persuading people to voluntarily mask themselves, while socially distancing from one another over a virus that has been revealed many times over to have less than one percent fatality rate. This was successful mostly because of the way the argument was framed. Persuaders appealed to the decency of human nature by suggesting wearing a mask was the best way to keep you from infecting other people. This worked because the news media was feeding a steady stream of propaganda suggesting you could be carrying the disease without showing any symptoms. Drawing from other theories of human behavior, (which will be shown later) they knew this would serve as a "higher virtue device" if you will.

In this chapter, the idea that our two major political parties are working together to advance an agenda while also manipulating our thoughts and behaviors was discussed. Carefully crafted fear messages, which play on our emotions, values, and beliefs are employed as a weapon of mass destruction against a largely, unknowing and trusting public. Most people cannot fathom that such manipulation would be used by people who are supposed to be acting in the defense of liberty and justice. Regrettably, most people will also reject this idea as a conspiracy theory even though they have no other explanation as to why our society is rapidly descending into chaos.

Chapter Two
Critical Theory and Education

Critical theory advances the conception of a critical and normative theory which is committed to emancipation from all forms of oppression, as well as to freedom, happiness, and a rational ordering of society. (Douglas Kelner, Sociological Perspectives)

Those seeking to transform America into a collectivist member of a globalist government know the best way to affect change is to target the nation's youth. Adolf Hitler, for example, understood this well and wrote that those who control the youth control the future. He believed controlling education ensured a loyal, obedient population.

There are many similarities between Germany's education system under Hitler and the one America has today. First, the curriculum is standardized and controlled from the top down. Even though U.S. Code 1232a prohibits federal control over education or any supervision over the curriculum, the federal government still wields tremendous power over what our children learn.

Much of this control revolves around federal programs that states willingly jump on board with, like the controversial common core standards adopted under the Obama administration. Common core essentially nationalized the curriculum under the brilliant propaganda campaign describing it as a program that increases college readiness.[31]

Common core standards made big news in the early days of Obama's presidency because it was changing the way kids were taught math. According to Alex Newman of the New American Magazine, Stanford University professor, Dr. James Milgram, who was a member of the common core validation committee, refused to sign off on the program because it reflected lower expectations.[32] This coincides with what Henry Burke stated about common core and the fallacy that it promotes college readiness. He stated the common core standards stopped after algebra 2 and high school students are not required to take the necessary classes which would prepare them for careers in stem (science, technology, engineering and mathematics) fields.[33] Furthermore, he states students who have not progressed past Algebra 2 in high school have less than a forty percent chance of earning a college degree.[34] In other words, common core seems to be lowering the standards. The same is true for English.

According to Newman, most of the required reading under common core standards has shifted away from literary classics to technical, informational manuals. California schools, for example, recently banned *To Kill a Mockingbird* and *Huckleberry Finn*, along with other classic works on the grounds they promoted racism.[35] According to the journal, *Educational Policy Analysis*[36] The National

Governors Association urged for the nationalization of common core standards by suggesting textbooks across the country, along with curriculum and testing materials, align with the program. This same journal also states there was less attention paid to developing solid standards of achievement instead of focusing on what they thought students should learn. What is it that they are supposed to learn? More on that later.

According to the report, *The Common Core Debacle*[37] by Theodore Rebarber, common core resulted from a four-decade effort to improve student achievement and make American students more competitive on a global scale. During this period there was a substantial improvement in performance for math and reading however, it was not occurring fast enough at the end of the nineties. This resulted in the states advocating for national standards. These standards, as hinted at earlier, were found by scholars and researchers to be lacking in global competitiveness and meaningful educational content. Ironically, Rebarber states that for the first time in the four-decade period where scores were at least slowly improving, there is now a substantial decline. What is even more disheartening, because the program was sold as one that develops career readiness standards for all students, the decline in scores is among those already considered the lowest scoring student populations in the country. In other words, common core is lowering achievement levels of the already lowest achievers. How does this help?

In some ways, it *could* be argued common core standards were developed to prepare students for so-called "college readiness." Going back to the question posed earlier, what are students supposed to be learning? America has seemingly awakened to the fact our universities are pushing an extreme, liberally biased agenda. From the explicit, inappropriate sexual education agenda, to pushing the idea that America is a racist, oppressive nation, the term college readiness could very well be reinterpreted as liberal indoctrination.

As an example, the transgender education agenda is not one which is taking place on the local level. It is fully sponsored by government (taxpayer) funded organizations and the National Education Association. In February of this past year, the NEA teamed up with the Human Rights Campaign to push the transgender education agenda by reading books about transgenderism to elementary school children[38]. This was done under the guise of reducing bullying against transgender students. This was the same tactic used in bringing the homosexual agenda in schools years prior. According to the journal *Traditional Values,*[39] homosexual activists like Gerald Hannon openly advocated getting into the public schools to teach children about homosexuality under the convenient guise of aids prevention.

Another example of the obvious attempts to indoctrinate our children into leftist thinking was the so-called 1619 project. This was an attempt to literally rewrite history from the perspective the United States was founded the day the first slave ships arrived in the year 1619.[40] This project awakened America in a big way to what is taking place in public education concerning theories like Critical Race theory, which are used to give unsuspecting children the impression their country, culture, and society in which they live, is hateful and bigoted. President Trump, and rightfully so, signed an executive order banning the use of Critical Race Theory in the federal government.[41] On November 2, 2020, he signed another establishing the 1776 commission allegedly promoting patriotic education while targeting CRT.[42]

While this is an action that certainly earned him some fanfare, it will have little effect. Mainly because his education secretary, Betsy DeVos, signed the United States onto the United Nations Sustainable Development education agenda which is designed to merge the U.S. into a global government by the year 2030[43].

This was one of those moments that represent the many contradictions of the Trump presidency. On one hand, he pulls out of the Paris climate change accord, putting on a good show for his supporters, and on the other, his administration does this. It will not matter what actions he takes promoting patriotic education. If we are still signed onto the U.N. agenda, our children will grow up believing the U.S. is responsible for climate change and they will be ready and willing to surrender their rights to promote sustainable development.

The truth, and it is a hard one to accept, is Donald Trump's executive order will do little to change education because things like Critical Race Theory are a larger part of something simply called, Critical Theory. Critical Theory is embedded in nearly every educational endeavor one can undertake. If you were to do a google scholar search of the term, you will see articles on critical theory in nursing, technology, communications, English and even mathematics. Story problems no longer focus on simply teaching the basics of adding and subtracting in practical, everyday scenarios, but now focus on socio-political issues.

In an article entitled *The sociopolitical turn in mathematics education*, published in the *Journal for research in mathematics education*, Rochelle Gutiérrez argues that the focus should no longer be on what minority students need to learn about math, but educators should ask what the power structures are behind these decisions, and, from whose perspective are minorities expected to learn math?[44]

The implications behind this argument suggest the power structure of the public-school system systematically denies minorities access to effective math education, and, they are forced to learn from the perspective of the dominant social group, which the left would argue is a form of oppression. She is arguing this from a critical theory perspective.

Critical Theory itself goes far beyond the mere teaching students America is racist. It is a theoretical framework, based on Marxist thinking, from which all social problems, power structures, and cultural issues are viewed. The purpose is to transform society and free people from the oppressive social and power structures which supposedly keep them oppressed. Writing for the journal *Sociological Perspectives*, Douglas Kelner states that "critical theory advances the conception of a critical and normative theory which is committed to emancipation from all forms of oppression, as well as to freedom, happiness, and a rational ordering of society."[45] In other words, critical theory is employed in our schools from the perspective that American society is oppressive, and the intent is to encourage students to think critically of our culture for the purpose of transforming it into something else. To put it even more simply, American culture is presented as a problem, and socialism is presented as a solution.

Critical Theory originated from the Frankfurt School of Social Research[46] and is designed to transform capitalist society into a full-fledged democracy. According to Bohman, any theory which questions a dominant power structure, i.e., feminist theory, queer identity theory, transgender theory, or critical race theory, as a few examples, falls under the guise of critical theory. The question is then, how did critical theory become so embedded in our education system?

The answer to that question can be a bit disheartening as it alludes to a deceptive pattern of change that goes unseen by most people. A pattern of change that no less is repeated as it is hidden by fancy-sounding names as our attention is diverted to something that seems more important. For instance, during President Trump's four years in office American's watched in shock as radical leftists burned our cities and attacked Trump supporters almost at will with no consequence. These actions blinded Americans to the unconstitutional actions taken by the Trump administration while reinforcing unquestionable support. Thus, keeping Americans divided into opposing groups. On one hand, they are feinting one strategy while carrying out another in the background. The 2020 presidential election is another good example. They deliberately showed the nation how corrupted and easily manipulated our election system is to get you, the voter, to lose faith and demand change.

To go back to the question of how critical theory became so prominent in our education system, we must go back to the Reagan administration.

Ronald Reagan will always be remembered among conservatives as the man who fixed America's broken economy, while also defeating Communism in the east. The fall of the Berlin Wall was the highlight of his achievements, signifying the fall of the Soviet Union and its tyrannical rule. This solidified Reagan's prominence and reputation as one of the greatest conservative presidents in American history. Unfortunately, this narrative does not represent reality but is more of an indication of the depths the communists were, and are, willing to go to deceive their enemies and lull them into submission. Ronald Reagan, after all, was an actor. He gave brilliant speeches which articulated the beliefs of the American people and the evils of communism. He was able to reflect the values American's held dear in a way no one has been able to do since.

Deception is the overall grand strategy of the left. According to Anatoliy Golitsyn, author of the book The Perestroika Deception,[47] the Soviet's view on planning and political strategy was far different from that of the United States. Americans understood strategy in the context of short-term goals which are immediately achievable. Comparatively speaking, the communists viewed strategy as a series of special maneuvers that guided their party over long periods, which were designed to help them achieve their goals of conquests. They were masters of misinformation tactics and a technique commonly known as controlling the opposition. One of these party lines and special maneuvers was creating the illusion that communism had died, and the Soviet Union had taken on capitalist reforms. In fact, Golitsyn implicitly states that the purpose was to use this illusion as a weapon against the west. The defeat of communism and their willingness to adopt capitalist reforms would cause the west to lower its guard. Golitsyn even predicted the Soviets would deliberately allow the Berlin Wall to be taken down as a means of deceiving the west and lulling them into submission.

In 1985, according to former head of the office of educational research at the Department of Education under the Regan administration, Charlotte Iserbyt,[48] President Reagan met with Mikhail Gorbachev and signed The *exchanges and cooperation in scientific, technical, education, cultural and other fields* agreement,[49] which allowed the communists to have influence in our classrooms.

> "The agreements call for Cooperation in the field of science and technology and additional agreements in other specific fields, including the humanities and social sciences; the facilitation of the exchange by appropriate organizations of educational and teaching materials, including textbooks, syllabi and curricula, materials on methodology, samples of teaching instruments and audiovisual aids, and the exchange of primary and secondary school textbooks and other teaching materials...the conducting of joint studies on textbooks between appropriate organizations in the United States and the Ministry of Education of the U.S.S.R." (Iserbyt, Soviets in the Classroom)

Critical Theory was brought into our classrooms through these agreements because it paved the way for Soviet educators to introduce their ideas on education. For instance, according to Iserbyt, the agreement resulted in the creation of groups like the Soviet American institute, which promoted new ways of thinking through critical theory. As hard as it may be to learn that Reagan, the greatest conservative president, signed these agreements, there is no other explanation how such an anti-American teaching tool would become so prominent. Unless of course, the government allowed it.

Whether or not Reagan himself understood the depths of the agreements he signed, or, if he was lured into it by the prospects of achieving world peace, is a fair question that may never be answered.

Critical Theory is hidden under the guise of critical thinking. Using this term, educators can convince gullible students that they are engaging in a critical, as in urgent or necessary, thought processes concerning social policy or cultural issues. They are being trained to criticize their country and as noted earlier, view other alternatives in a more favorable light. Textbooks are controlled by propagandists who are highly trained in framing issues in a way that guides students' thinking towards a desired end. Socialist solutions are presented as being the only way to solve America's problems. Textbooks are written purposefully to discredit our culture, history, and achievements as a nation. Most frightening of all is their intent to present freedom as an unworkable concept that is responsible for the problems we currently face.

The desired result is a demoralized population. One that has lost its identity and is not motivated to continue in the system that has sustained it because it is now viewed as immoral, selfish, and corrupted. American's have taken great pride in their national identity. We believe all people have inalienable rights and have demonstrated repeatedly, that we are willing to fight for the freedom of others. Using critical theory to make young children question their nation' s values, serves to destroy this sense of national morality while also destroying the human soul itself. Nathaniel Branden writes in his essay *The Psychology of Pleasure*[50] that the erosion of man's soul will result in the eventual destruction of all motivation to achieve anything at all. Americans have created perhaps the strongest economic engine in existence. By equating capitalism with selfishness and bigotry, through the lens of critical theory, the left is successfully destroying man's motivation to continue in this system. They are as Alinsky says, creating a sense of hopelessness in the current system so a new one will be readily accepted in its place.

Chapter Three
Socializing American Students

Moral individualism is set up by the conscious separation of different centers of life. It has its roots in the notion that the consciousness of each person is wholly private, a self-enclosed continent, intrinsically independent of the ideas, wishes, purposes of everybody else. (John Dewey, Democracy and Education)

Not only are our children having their values destroyed by critical theory, but new values and the negative feelings associated with their country are being reinforced through operant conditioning techniques employed in the classroom. Operant conditioning is a series of behavior reinforcement measures designed to encourage desired behaviors and discourage undesired behaviors. In other words, children's change in attitude, and the acceptance of new behaviors are being rewarded with praise by the teacher, making the student feel more accepted.

In 1969, the U.S. Department of Health, Education, and Welfare released a booklet titled *Reducing Behavior Problems: An Operant Conditioning Guide for Children,*[51] where it is stated in the abstract that the purpose is to change undesirable behaviors in children. This is not to say children fail to display behavior in the classroom which is unconducive to a learning environment. Behavior modification is acceptable in certain circumstances, however; operant conditioning is being used to reinforce new values, change morals, and at the very least, silence opposing voices. Children are being rewarded with praise for looking at new perspectives on their traditionally held beliefs presented to them through critical theory. It is a one-two punch that children have no idea they are being hit with.

A good example is when I was a student at Northeastern State University and our professor subtlety introduced the concept of white privilege. The conversation was innocent enough, and most people probably had no idea their thoughts were being shaped by it. While discussing the election of 2008, she asked how many students' grandparents did not vote for Obama. A sizable portion of the class raised their hands. She then asked if it was possible their refusal to do so was motivated by racism. At first, this took the class by surprise, but when the professor reinforced the suggestion with a funny racist joke about old white people, the class relaxed and accepted it as a possibility. This little scenario opened the door for these students to change their perspective on the country they live in and, the culture they are a part of.

Most people make the simple and innocent assumption education is designed to mold children into successful free thinkers, able to navigate themselves through a competitive and chaotic world. While at one time this may have been true, it has progressed into something far different where the aim is to create a new social consciousness, a society that sees socialism as the best alternative to man's social problems. The goal of education today is to create a society ready to merge into a new global order.

Charlotte Iserbyt, in her book *The Deliberate Dumbing Down of America,* cites a speech given by Augustus Thomas, from 1927. Thomas was the education commissioner for the state of Maine at the time. He believed that education should be used to shape and change values in a way that moves us from the undesirable adherence to nationalism, to a new international morality. He acknowledged this would be a long process of educating generations of people to accept this new perspective.

"If there are those who think we are to jump immediately into a new world order, actuated by complete understanding and brotherly love, they are doomed to disappointment. If we are ever to approach that time, it will be after patient and persistent effort of long duration. The present international situation of mistrust and fear can only be corrected by a formula of equal status, continuously applied, to every phase of international contacts, until the cobwebs of the old order are brushed out of the minds of the people of all lands. This means that the world must await a long process of education and a building up of public conscience and an international morality, or, in other words, until there is a worldwide sentiment which will back up the modern conception of a world community. This brings us to the international mind, which is nothing more or less than the habit of thinking of foreign relations and business affecting the several countries of the civilized world as free co-operating equals."[52]

For the past one hundred years, America's education system has been working to shape the morals and values of students in a way which makes them see their culture and world view in a negative light. John Dewey, known as the father of modern education, was instrumental in the creation of this new education. Dewey was a Fabian socialist and author of the Humanist Manifesto. Humanist philosophy puts man and his accomplishments at the center of everything as it denies the existence of a supreme being.

Fabianism is a more incremental approach to implementing socialism without the need for a violent revolution,[53] mostly through democratic methods. One of the key methods of the Fabians is to use propaganda to convince men of the evils of capitalism and promote socialist ideas.[54] It could be reasonably suggested the Fabian socialists adopted the use of critical theory in education, not just in America but around the world, to turn people's thinking toward socialism.

John Dewey, being a Fabian socialist, believed there was a need to move away from a traditional education where reading, arithmetic, and writing were the focus as society progressed into the industrial age. He saw the old systems and institutions which revolved around the family and the church as crumbling and outdated, not able to fulfill the needs of the new developing society. Science, the arts, and nature learning would take precedence. Education should focus on socializing the student opposed to educating them to be free thinkers. Dewey believed a public education system, where schooling was free, and children were guided by trained teachers, had the potential to create a system where the children themselves would be aiding in the creation of an egalitarian society. In *Democracy and Education,* John Dewey wrote the following on his views of socialized education —

"When the social quality of individualized mental operations is denied, it becomes a problem to find connections which will unite an individual with his fellows. Moral individualism is set up by the conscious separation of different centers of life. It has its roots in the notion that the consciousness of each person is wholly private, a self-enclosed continent, intrinsically independent of the ideas, wishes, purposes of everybody else. A being whose activities are associated with others has a social environment. What he does and what he can do depend upon the expectations, demands, approvals, and condemnations of others. A being connected with other beings cannot perform his own activities without taking the activities of others into account. For they are the indispensable conditions of the realization of his tendencies."[55]

What Dewey is essentially arguing is the precept of individualism, a system of morals based on the principles of individual liberty, is not conducive to a productive society and, a person's accomplishments are not his or hers alone, but products of the collective society. Sounds like something we heard during the Obama administration, doesn't it? This is essentially the same as Marx saying, "from each according to their ability, to each according to their need." The only difference is it is not accomplished by force rather, people are trained to accept this through public schooling. It is being done using operant conditioning. As noted earlier, behavioral and attitude changes towards values that promote socialist ideas, are being rewarded with reinforcement techniques that make students feel they are doing the right thing.

Operant conditioning is a theory of behavior modification first put forth by behavioral psychologist, B.F. Skinner. Skinner was also an atheist who believed that man had no will of his own and behavior is largely a product of our environment. In the book *Science and Human Behavior* Skinner alludes to the idea that man is not in control of his behavior but, once certain environmental conditions are met, his actions can be largely predicted and controlled. He also believed that science had gone as far as it can go in its quest to control nature and a science of human behavior was necessary to reign in our insatiable appetite for power and control.

Our nature is destructive in some ways, whereas the development of industry led to the creation of nuclear weapons capable of destroying the world several times over on one hand, and on the other, can leave millions of people without work as technology advances, leaving people to suffer and go hungry. It is for these reasons Skinner believed it was necessary to apply a standard of study to human behavior, a model that would guide the examination of all human actions from the same perspective. This perspective was human beings had no will of their own, and we are easily controlled by the conditions of our environment. If the environment and the circumstances around an individual can be controlled, so too can the individual.

> "If we are to use the methods of science in the field
> of human affairs, we must assume that behavior is
> lawful and determined. We must expect to discover
> that what a man does is the result of specifiable
> conditions and that once these conditions have

been discovered, we can anticipate and to some extent determine his actions. This possibility is offensive to many people. It is opposed to a tradition of long standing which regards man as a free agent, whose behavior is the product, not of specifiable antecedent conditions, but of spontaneous inner changes of course. Prevailing philosophies of human nature recognize an internal *will* which has the power of interfering with causal relationships, and which makes the prediction and control of behavior impossible. To suggest that we abandon this view is to threaten many cherished beliefs—to undermine what appears to be a stimulating and productive conception of human nature."[56]

John Dewey and B.F. Skinner were alike in the sense they both viewed man as needing social conditioning for a new world. Dewey believed that education could be used to socialize students into becoming a globalized citizen and Skinner developed the method for which it could happen. The use of operant conditioning as a behavior change strategy is based on a very thorough understanding of a basic human need. The need to fit in and be a part of the group.

Theoretically, there is nothing wrong with correcting behavior using this method with a child exhibiting problematic behaviors if all other attempts have failed. The

Operant Conditioning guide for Teachers,[57] for example, makes a great point by saying we are all motivated by a system of rewards and punishment. Teachers are inspired to teach because they receive the payoff, or the reward, of knowing that their students are learning something useful. Everyone who receives a paycheck is responding to this reward by continuing to go to work. To use operant conditioning to change behaviors and beliefs, on the other hand, is a different story. This is what is happening.

Human beings have a need to be socially accepted. No one likes to be isolated and left to feel alone. In *Beyond Freedom and Dignity*[58] Skinner states that the desire to fit in can be more of a controlling influence than a full-blown police state. People have a fear of being disapproved of in social settings. Imagine a child in elementary school being asked to express an opinion, or even share their parents' unpopular beliefs on a certain topic. Then imagine a disapproving tone and the feeling of being singled out and humiliated as the reinforcement technique to change behavior. Now, imagine that going on from kindergarten through college.

Admittedly, Skinner states that this is not always guaranteed to change opinions or beliefs as much as it is behavior. He acknowledges man's ability to resist. This is strange because man would have to have a will of his own and demonstrate control of his behavior to do so, and Skinner does not believe we are capable of that. In a school system designed to push globalist ideals, filled with teachers hostile toward American values, constant reinforcement by singling out those who refuse to go along will at the very least, keep them quiet and afraid to express their beliefs. Which as far as their concerned, is good enough.

While Skinner did note this was no guarantee of attitude change, there have been studies suggesting verbal reinforcement cues can be effective in changing not only behaviors but attitudes as well. An article entitled *Verbal reinforcement of attitude* [59] in the Journal of *Personality and social psychology*, found that using the word good in response to test subjects' answers to survey questions was enough to see a change in attitude that lasted at least over a week. Another study entitled *Cognitive consequences of forced compliance*[60] in the *Journal of abnormal and social psychology*, suggests that people's opinions and attitudes can be changed when forced to argue for the opinion they generally disagree with. If a child in middle school, for example, is singled out for expressing views skeptical of climate change, then asked to write a paper supporting it, and given a great grade and praised for the work, he or she is more likely to have a shift in opinion because the child now feels accepted. Again, imagine the schedules of reinforcement and the same type of conditioning occurring over the years the child is attending school. These are vague examples; however, it is what is happening in our government-controlled education system. The question is whether there is a real change in belief, or if the child is just being trained to be compliant. Either way, it serves the ends of those working to create a consciousness suitable to globalism.

Another aspect of Skinner's theories bearing relevance to behavioral change is referred to as effort justification, which will be mentioned again later in greater detail. Though the term itself aligns more with Festinger's[61] theory of cognitive dissonance, which states that people will naturally seek ways to alleviate feelings of psychological discomfort when behaviors do not align with beliefs. It is the type of inconsistency in behaviors that do not align with the person's attitudes or opinions, or knowledge pertaining to such behavior that defines cognitive dissonance.

Dissonance is the feeling that occurs when the individual attempts to rationalize away their own blaring inconsistencies, due to the psychological discomfort the contradiction causes. Effort justification then, is the natural tendency humans have, to assign high value to their efforts. Let's go back to the middle school student being asked to write a paper that contradicts his or her previous beliefs. It has already been demonstrated that simply being made to write the paper may lead to a change in opinion. Imagine then, the child being praised for the hard work that was put into writing it, this effort will be the justification for the change of attitude, to alleviate the discomfort of the contradiction.

I witnessed this taking place in the college classroom as a student in the social work program I mentioned. All the students were asked to write a paper describing their beliefs about white privilege, and how they did not realize the effects of their own racism. After the paper was turned in and graded, the students were then made to stand in front of the class and cite the reasons they were racist and benefited from white privilege. They all complied with the assignment, and for the rest of the semester no one spoke out against the concept of systematic racism. This is because they were all praised for their efforts and, their attitude changes towards the subject.

While many of the students may have not changed their beliefs, they changed their behavior and justified it because of the hard work they put into the assignment. Just like the fear of not fitting in, it is a natural human tendency to value the work we do. This implies the idea there is a certain virtue attached to the work. It could then be theorized that this is where the term virtue signaling comes from. People are controlled by the idea they are acting out of a higher sense of virtue than others and it is this sense of moral superiority which alleviates the dissonance between belief and behavior. Interestingly enough, and this will be discussed again later, we see this concept playing out today as we deal with mask mandates and forced shutdowns in response to a virus with a .26 percent fatality rate.

This chapter attempted to draw correlations between critical theory, the ideas of John Dewey, and the science of human behavior. It is being theorized that critical theory is used to introduce students to a new way of thinking and, operant conditioning is then being used to reward attitude and behavioral changes that align with socialist goals. While it is just a theory of my own based on an understanding of my own research and experiences, there is the question of why our students are graduating top-tier universities hating their country and demanding socialism. The information presented in this chapter at least lays a theoretical approach as to how it could be happening.

Chapter Four
Drugged into Compliance

Stimulant drugs have two basic effects on animals and children regardless of their mental status. First. stimulants reduce all spontaneous and social behavior. This makes the child more docile. submissive. and manageable (compliant). Second. stimulants enforce perseverative. obsessive-compulsive. or over-focused behavior. (Dr. Peter Breggin: What psychologists and therapists need to know about ADHD and stimulants)

Another interesting correlation between education and the changing attitudes of our youth is the fact since 1987,[62] millions of school children have been labeled with a mental condition known as Attention Deficit Hyperactivity Disorder. These children are prescribed powerful drugs to control their behavior.

One such drug is Ritalin. Ritalin is a schedule II narcotic, a controlled substance that has the same effects on the mind as cocaine. It is highly addictive and has been known to cause severe problems for children taking it. These problems include psychological conditions which could lead to more drug use such as suicidal or homicidal thoughts, depression, and cognitive impairment.[63] Other side effects include but are not limited to, cardiovascular and heart problems and involuntary shaking.

ADHD as a disease is difficult to identify. In fact, several people in the psychiatric profession take the position that (as defined), the disease simply does not exist.[64] ADHD is considered a set of symptoms including forgetfulness, inability to sit still and pay attention for long periods of time, being easily distracted, and always being in a rush. Symptoms any one of us could show at any time during our busy days. Displaying these symptoms for a period of six months is often all it takes to be labeled as having ADHD.[65]

The problem with identifying a disease based solely on the existence of symptoms is that there is no evidence that a biological disease is causing them.[66] This is true for almost all mental disorders as well. For years, the term chemical imbalance has been used to describe almost all psychological problems. This theory first came about in the sixties when Thorazine, the commonly prescribed drug for mental illness at the time, was found to block the brain's dopamine production.[67] While many still cling to this chemical imbalance theory, there is no evidence it is true. In fact, existing evidence suggests the use of psychiatric medicines in the first place, is the cause for chemical imbalances in the brain. This in turn, leads to a need for more medicines.[68]

The idea of ADHD being a fraudulent disease is not some narrow-minded conspiracy theory. Given the millions of children being prescribed drugs like Ritalin, you would expect there to be a rigorous testing process to verify a child has it before being given drugs at all. There is not.[69] In many cases, all it takes is a simple recommendation by a teacher based on their observations of the child's behavior.[70] In other words, if the teacher feels a child is being disruptive or is unable to sit still well enough, they can bring this up to the school's counselor or social worker and the child will be evaluated for ADHD.

This evaluation is not a biological test looking for a physical anomaly that is present with other diseases. Instead, it is based on simple observations of behavior. A psychologist or social worker may also rely on interviews with other people familiar with the child and psychological assessments to make their determination.

There are other motivating factors, besides behavior, which drive ADHD diagnosis as well. For instance, psychologists were curious as to why there was such a discrepancy in ADHD rates across the country. What they found was a correlation between states with high diagnosis' and laws that hold school districts accountable for high failure rates.[71] Once a student has been diagnosed with ADHD their academic records are no longer figured into the assessment. This gives school districts a financial incentive to identify children they can diagnose with ADHD because higher failure rates equal less funding.

Another motivating factor is profit for the pharmaceutical companies. According to a study that was published in the *Journal of the American Medical Association*,[72] more than half of the doctors in the United States received kickbacks from pharmaceutical companies and makers of medical devices for using or prescribing their products. The total uncovered was over two billion dollars.

This does not just pertain to the prescribing of Ritalin but is a practice that is occurring all throughout the medical profession. What is most disconcerting, however, is the direct financial ties between the pharmaceutical companies who manufacture psychiatric medicines and the so-called doctors who are responsible for defining the symptoms and conditions for mental disorders. According to the article *Financial Ties between DSM-IV panel members and the pharmaceutical industry*,[73] over half of the doctors who sit on the DSM advisory board are taking direct payments from drug manufacturers. The DSM is the Diagnostic and Statistical Manual of mental health disorders. The advisory panel is where mental health disorders are voted into existence and added to the manual based only on vague ideas of symptoms, not hard scientific data.[74] In other words, those taking direct payments are likely being influenced on how to define certain mental health conditions by the pharmaceutical companies.

Is it possible that drugs like Ritalin are being prescribed not to treat a disease but to induce compliance and encourage attitude change? A theory called induced compliance posits the idea that positive or negative emotions, presented in association with information that contradicts one's views, are powerful factors in changing attitudes.

In an article entitled *Induced-compliance attitude change: once more with feeling,*[75] published in *The Journal of experimental psychology* in 1979, the authors cited a study in which stimulants or tranquilizers were given to students while being asked to write essays which countered their typical beliefs. It was found that students who were given the stimulants were very easily persuaded to change their position while those given the tranquilizers, were not. From this experiment, social scientists came to believe when people are under the influence of a stimulant, their attitudes and beliefs can be easily changed. It is reasonable to conclude that a restless child who is not complying with classroom etiquette would be quickly referred to a school counselor for a behavioral evaluation. If their behavior is deemed intolerable, they will be prescribed Ritalin.

Another study involving the writing of essays that countered the subject's beliefs was conducted with the use of caffeinated beverages. Caffeine is a stimulant. It was found that attitude change and persuasion were more likely to occur due to the increased systematic processing of the arguments being presented, after moderate doses of caffeine, leading to higher rates of agreement.[76]

Dr. Peter Breggin writes in his paper *What psychologists and therapists need to know about ADHD and stimulants,*[77] that stimulant use in children suppresses the natural inclination to be active, social, innovative, and curious about learning. In animals, the use of Ritalin, according to Breggin, resulted in passively accepting captivity as opposed to trying to escape a caged environment.

Animals under the influence of stimulants generally engage in useless repetitive behaviors or simply stare off into space. This is due to an effect like the one demonstrated by the caffeine studies. Over-focused behavior due to higher systematic processing of information. It becomes obsessive-compulsive type behavior. According to Breggin, repressive behaviors such as compliance and reduced curiosity are common in children taking stimulant drugs. Unfortunately, because the drugs are typically prescribed to reign in what is viewed as inattentive or disruptive behavior, these effects are typically considered an improvement in behavior.

> "Stimulant drugs have two basic effects on animals and children regardless of their mental status. First. stimulants reduce all spontaneous and social behavior. This makes the child more docile. submissive. and manageable (compliant). Second. stimulants enforce perseverative. obsessive-compulsive. or over-focused behavior. This makes the child more easily led or compelled to do role. boring activities. These twin toxic effects are readily misinterpreted as 'improved behavior' in highly structured or controlled environments where children are given insufficient or inappropriate

attention. and where their genuine needs are being ignored. As a result of toxicity, stimulants suppress a child's behavior in a global fashion that has nothing to do with any diagnosis or disorder."[78]

The larger point of Dr. Breggin's paper is medications like Ritalin are being prescribed at an alarming rate. In fact, most of the recommendations for its use are coming from our public schools. Is it being done on purpose to create a more compliant student? Or are teachers and school counselors just misinformed about the drug's real effects? There is some evidence that suggests doctors not only understand the effects of Ritalin but, advocate for their use because of these effects.

Psychologist Christian Perring wrote an article in the journal *Bioethics* entitled *Medicating children: The case for Ritalin.*[79] She argues the drug should be used not only on children displaying ADHD-type symptoms but, on children and parents who are willing to take the risks because of the drug's behavioral changing attributes. In fact, on the second page of the article she makes a startling comment suggesting that drugs are indeed used to control behavior and *form the minds of children.*

"So, the issue of Ritalin's use is fairly new in biomedical ethics and promises to be an issue of increasing importance as people become more concerned about its use, *and new drugs are developed which will be more sophisticated in their ability to control and form the minds of children.* It is important that we find the right questions to ask, and the right language to use in framing the discussion of these issues."[80]

She suggests framing the argument in a way that alleviates the fears people have over the use of psychotropic medications. She also argues that the concerns of a child being labeled with a mental disorder should be alleviated by the idea the drug improves school performance. This chapter has demonstrated that this is not the case, these drugs do not improve school performance. Most interestingly, she attempts to discredit the concerns that Ritalin may be used to induce compliance of the child as a form of thought control. She freely admits that the drug changes behavior but contests the idea that these behavior changes should be associated with thought control any more than what the teacher is teaching the child through the normal course of the day.

Therein lies the issue, the drug is meant to control the child and increase compliance with the teacher's instructions. It may not change their opinions or beliefs, but if it controls their behavior to the point where they become agreeable, and simply go along to get along, the mission has been accomplished. Imagine being on such a drug throughout your entire duration of formal schooling.

In 1967, a meeting was held in Puerto Rico among the world's top mental health experts to discuss the growing field of psychotropic drug use.[81] It was recognized that there was a potential to use these drugs as a means of subduing the human will and controlling our cognitive functioning and emotional status. In fact, according to the Citizens Commission on Human Rights, the potential these drugs held was discussed in relation to creating a utopian state of mind, one where man would be more willing to accept a new society.

As conspiratorial as it sounds the meeting did occur and it was concluded that the use of psychiatric drugs could indeed suppress the human will to act and, affect our mental abilities to the point of mindless compliance. According to Licensed Clinical Social Worker Mark Ruffalo[82] the growth and popularity of psychotropic drug use can be attributed to Dr. Nathan S. Kline who is thought to be the pioneer in psychopharmacology. Ruffalo attributes the following quote to Kline.

> "Those of us who work in this field see a developing potential for nearly total control of human emotional status, mental functioning, and the will to act. These human phenomena can be started, stopped or eliminated by the use of various types of chemical substances. What we can produce with our science now will affect the entire society."

There is some confusion as to where this quote originated. The Citizens Commission of Human Rights video "Making a Killing" attributes it to Dr. Wayne Evans while Ruffalo at Psychology Today, cites Kline. The quote also appeared in an issue of Fortune Magazine at one time, so it was said. It is also clear that the use of these drugs is creating an attitude of compliance along with an impairment in cognitive functioning. Sometimes, truth speaks for itself.

We are living in a time where it seems the ability to reason for oneself is a diminishing attribute, and the willingness to just go along with the perceived norm is increasingly becoming common place. The so-called Covid-19 pandemic and the mass compliance with unnecessary mask mandates is a good example. Is there a relationship between this and the use of drugs such as Ritalin? The Citizens Commission on Human Rights reports that as many as seventy-eight million Americans are taking some type of psychiatric medicine[83] and, almost seven million of these people are younger than seventeen years old.

An article entitled *An ethical analysis of contemporary use of coercive persuasion (Brainwashing and Mind Control) in psychiatry*[84] suggests the use of these drugs is in fact, little more than a coercive attempt to change people's behaviors and attitudes. The psychiatric profession is geared towards the changing of behavior in people who are exhibiting real signs of mental illness, or self-destructiveness. In most cases, however, people are prescribed powerful, life altering drugs under the false pretext that they are treating a biological anomaly causing a disease when they are not. Just as it is the case with ADHD, there is no identifiable disease with alleged conditions like depression or anxiety. These conditions are emotional states of mind that are being treated like a disease for profit and control.

Thomas Szasz[85] explains it by saying diseases of the body, which exist biologically, manifest themselves in an identifiable way, while behaviors that are attributed to mental illness show no signs of existence except through behaviors. Psychiatric drugs then, according to Ventegodt et al,[86] do little to treat these conditions while making it extremely difficult to not cooperate with suggestive persuasion techniques. In other words, the drugs are pacifying people, making them obedient.

Another interesting correlation, albeit a more sensitive and controversial one, is the rise of marijuana use in the United States. Almost overnight, medical marijuana became a sensation and states are increasingly legalizing its recreational use. In fact, On Friday, December 4, 2020, the House of Representatives passed a bill that would legalize it nationally and expunge the records of those charged with marijuana crimes. For many people who consider themselves patriots and advocates for constitutional rights, this is a win.

The argument has revolved around the rights of government to regulate a plant, which many people feel has health benefits. To be fair, there is evidence that in some cases, marijuana use can alleviate pain associated with arthritis and nerve damage; however, it has always been listed as a schedule 1 drug. Meaning there was no recognizable medical benefits to its use.

Unfortunately, there is a reason to speculate that the legalization of marijuana is being done because the powers that be understand its hypnotic properties. While there has not been many studies examining the effects of marijuana on user's susceptibility to persuasion, compared to the use of LSD, for example, there is evidence suggesting the use of marijuana has the same effects as other psychotropic drugs. The article *Marijuana use and hypotonic susceptibility*[87] show there is a relationship between the effects of marijuana and the user's responsiveness to persuasive communication strategies. In other words, when people are high, they are more likely to simply go along with the program. This should be concerning to all Americans. Unfortunately, the high that comes from smoking pot is powerful and causes feelings of euphoria along with an increased sense of awareness. Some people feel like they are better at whatever they are doing when under the influence of marijuana. There is simply too much evidence showing the impairment of cognitive functioning, increased hostility, and development of psychosis to go into here.

Given the fact that most Americans have mindlessly complied with the hysterical mandates associated with

Covid-19, they should be, in the interest of defending their own liberty, interested to see if there is a correlation between this compliance and drug use. They are not. In fact, if you were to mention the possibility you would probably be labeled as a conspiracy theorist. It is important to understand, however, that drug use affects people in different ways. Not everyone under the influence of a depression medicine, for example, is easily persuadable if rooted in their convictions.

Chapter Five
A Science with no Morality

Like Darwin, Marx thought he had discovered the law of development. He saw history in stages, as the Darwinists saw geological strata and successive forms of life. Both Marx and Darwin made struggle the means of development. (Jacques Barzun, Darwin, Marx, Wagner: Critique of a Heritage)

Thus far we have discussed some theories and ideas as to why our kids are so readily accepting or demanding socialism. The main idea is persuasive communication messages, along with critical theory and operant conditioning, are being used to change opinions and attitudes in school children. The idea drugs are being intentionally prescribed to children, knowing they produce a state of mindless compliant behavior, was also discussed. In this chapter, we will be revisiting and diving deeper into something mentioned earlier. B.F. Skinner's science of human behavior and its relation to communism. This is important and will come into sharper focus as our discussion shifts gears towards Covid-19 and what is known about compliance in later chapters.

Skinner was a pioneer in the development of behavioral sciences. He standardized the examination of human behavior by suggesting it be viewed strictly from a scientific viewpoint as opposed to a spiritual one. To Skinner, our actions were not the result of free choice or the control of our own will, but the result of environmental circumstances which he claims can be traced back to our evolutionary past.

There are major implications to believing man has no control over his own will. Implications which tie into another philosophy which relates to human behavior, Darwinism. Skinner says in *Beyond Freedom and Dignity* that behavior should be viewed from a scientific as opposed to a pre-scientific view. This means that before Darwin, it was believed that man had control over his thoughts and actions, and it was his free will that could be attributed to all his behaviors. After Darwin, man becomes nothing more than just another animal, a more evolved ape with no soul or will of his own.

> "In what we may call the pre-scientific view (and the word is not necessarily pejorative) a person's behavior is at least to some extent his own achievement. He is free to deliberate, decide, and act, possibly in original ways, and he is to be given credit for his successes and blamed for his failures. In the scientific view (and the word is not necessarily honorific) a person's behavior is determined by a genetic endowment traceable to the evolutionary history of the species and by the environmental circumstances to which as an

individual he has been exposed. Neither view can be proved, but it is in the nature of scientific inquiry that the evidence should shift in favor of the second. As we learn more about the effects of the environment, we have less reason to attribute any part of human behavior to an autonomous controlling agent. And the second view shows a marked advantage when we begin to do something about behavior. Autonomous man is not easily changed: in fact, to the extent that he is autonomous, he is by definition, not changeable at all. But the environment can be changed, and we are learning how to change it. The measures we use are those of physical and biological technology, but we use them in special ways to affect behavior."[88]

Skinner is laying out the argument that any inquiry into human behavior should be done from a scientific view because it enables them to do more when it comes to controlling behavior. It does not take the application of science to realize that an individual's environment is going to influence their choices and actions; however, making a science out of learning to manipulate the environment denies man his free will. This is exactly what Skinner is saying.

Looking back at previous chapters we have seen through critical theory, punishment-reward systems of control, and the use of drugs, that the environment is very much being manipulated with the intent of controlling every aspect of our lives.

Are there moral implications to this? It is one thing to use a tool like operant conditioning, for example, to change the behavior of someone experiencing emotional trauma or, a criminal in some type of rehabilitation program. To use it on school children for the purpose of controlling and changing attitudes is another issue altogether.

Morality itself is being twisted in this discussion because the very definitions of the word between those believing in this type of approach to understanding behavior, and those adhering to the traditional ideas of morality, are vastly different. To assume man has no control over his behavior, or to base a science of understanding human beings on this idea, falls in line with Darwinism and his theory of evolution. If man is viewed as an animal instead of a spiritual being created by God, then it is reasonable to assume man's behavior would have to be controlled and any means in doing so would be justified. Including the drugging of children to induce compliance with state objectives.

In the book *Created from animals: The moral implications of Darwinism*,[89] James Rachels argues because humans evolved from primates, we are entitled to no more rights or privileges than any other animal. Though he does acknowledge a difference between men and animals, he posits the idea that a morality less centered on man being superior to animals is called for. He argues that the notion of human dignity and morality, based on the previously believed notion of the existence of God has changed because Darwin's theory allegedly proves the existence of man is accidental and without special purpose. A new morality based on the concepts of evolution, where the value of life should no longer be defined by an unprovable God, but by us, is now needed. This is humanism in a nutshell.

If this is the view that Skinner held when developing a science of behavior, then there would indeed be moral implications. It means man exists without a moral compass and that we are nothing but an empty slate. If men are defining the terms of right and wrong, moral and immoral, and the values we should adhere to, can they not decide who and who does not have the right to exist based on who conforms to these standards?

Under the philosophy known as moral individualism, which is what Rachels argues should be the outlook taken by Darwinists, it is justifiable to treat people differently based on their characteristics. Using medical experiments involving chimpanzees as an example, he makes the argument that automatically viewing the chimp's life as being less valuable than a human's is misguided because we share many of the same characteristics. If it were determined that the chimp possessed individual characteristics which were more desirable than the human's, it would be justified to perform the medical experiments on the human instead. He also argues that equality between people is misguided because we are in fact, not equal.

People are different, this is true. What is lacking from this perspective is the definition of equality from the Christian view. Or, from the American view of equality under the law or, of opportunity. These aspects are missing from his equation because the idea of God, or of man having a special purpose has already been rejected. This is the first moral implication of evolution.

Rachels' argument revolves around the idea of justifying the different treatment of individuals based on their relevant differences and, a theory describing this justification is needed. The problem is there exists no higher moral standard that is being used to judge, it is now left in the hands of men to define morality and values. Under the notions of Biblical equality, people are all equal under God. Under the notions of equality of opportunity, people are all able to use their natural talents to pursue happiness. Under the notion of equality under the law, people all have the same civil rights and are treated equally in the legal system regardless of class, age, race, or gender. Under Rachels' moral individualism, treating people differently is justified based on their relevant differences.

What are the relevant differences that Rachels refers to? Consider the main topic of discussion in this book. There is a deliberate effort to change the opinions and attitudes of people in this country to be more accepting of socialism. A system that is presented as morally superior where people freely share their wealth for the betterment of the community and those who are opposed are referred to as, in the words of Hillary Clinton, deplorables.

Over the years, conservatives in America have been portrayed as selfish, uncompassionate, racist, greedy, and even mentally ill because of our so-called, resistance to change.[90] Is it possible that they would justify the different treatment of people based on a moral system created entirely by man, and completely devoid of God? This is what Rachels is arguing, and it has led to some of the biggest atrocities the world has known.

According to the *Black Book of Communism*[91] the mass murders committed by the communist regimes of the early twentieth century were driven by an urge to reshape human nature. This explains why there is such an apologetic attitude towards communism. They were attempting to, so they claimed, create a world of total equality based on the notion everyone worked for the betterment of everybody else. The producing classes, in the view of the communists, were the oppressors. Failing to conform to this new way of thinking was often viewed as a form of mental illness. Why would you not want to conform to a system of fairness and equality?

Most people remember the genocide committed by Adolf Hitler. It was perhaps the most ruthless in the sense that it deliberately targeted a specific race of people for extermination. This is the very definition of genocide. When compared to the motivations of the communists,

Nazism appears on the surface, to be the evilest of the two. Though, Hitler and the Communists were driven by the same ideological underpinnings, Darwinism.

Karl Marx was enthralled by Darwin's theories. In fact, evolution was a fundamental philosophy contributing to Marx's development of communism. It provided the necessary, *scientific rationale* that justified the denial of God.[92] Marx saw that he could turn the pursuit of egalitarian communism into a scientific endeavor by relating his theory to evolution. He believed life was a class a struggle and, just as Darwin explained evolution occurring through material conflict, Marx believed humanity could evolve into something more perfect through a clash between the haves and have nots.

> "Like Darwin, Marx thought he had discovered the law of development. He saw history in stages, as the Darwinists saw geological strata and successive forms of life. Both Marx and Darwin made struggle the means of development. Again, the measure of value in Darwin is survival with reproduction—an absolute fact occurring in time and which wholly disregards the moral or esthetic quality of the product. In Marx, the measure of value is expended labor—an absolute fact occurring in time, which also disregards the utility of the product. Both Darwin and Marx [also] tended to hedge and

modify their mechanical absolution in the face of objections."[93]

Much more could be said about the development of communism and the concepts of class struggle. For example, the Hegelian Dialectic is often referred to as the problem-reaction-solution strategy. It is central to the advancement of communism in any society, as it works off the concept that progress happens through conflict. Many people believe problems are deliberately created with the purpose of manipulating the public into demanding a predetermined solution.

The point of this chapter, however, is to draw awareness to the consequences of developing a science of human behavior. Skinner's ideas were largely based on the idea that man had no will of his own and that his behavior could be largely controlled by his surrounding environment. If there is an effort to condition or persuade people into changing their opinions, attitudes, and beliefs to be more favorable towards a collective society, what are the consequences when these efforts fail? If man has no special purpose and is just an accident of evolution, there is nothing stopping the justification of treating people differently if their behavior cannot be changed in a favorable way. If men and animals are to be treated as equals, then there would be no moral objections to eliminating populations of people who fail to align their beliefs and values to state objectives.

The biggest problem with Skinner's theory is the denial of truth. The urge to study human behavior from a scientific point of view is driven by nothing more than an urge to control human behavior. Even Skinner acknowledges that beliefs are not as easily controlled or changed as a behavior because people have an ability to resist.[94]

If man had no will, as Darwinism suggests, then controlling behavior would not require such an effort. Men would not be able to resist behavioral change strategies. It is this resistance that such efforts to manipulate the minds and actions of men are geared, to lessen their ability to do so.

When it comes to the issue of changing opinions or behaviors, Skinner says the use of a stimulus that changes the environment only has partial control and there are other ways of reinforcing behavioral change. Stimuli that are associated with negative or positive consequences which are built upon an individual's natural tendency to act in a certain way are also effective.

Persuasive techniques, when there is a desire to get someone to act in a certain way, for example, are more effective when a positive consequence is attached to it. Go back to the seven-year-old sitting in the classroom being rewarded for agreeing with the teacher's ideas of Critical Race Theory and America as a racist nation. Rewarding, or punishing someone based on their compliance is the basis of Skinner's science of human behavior.

Recall the quote from Skinner's *Beyond Freedom and Dignity* where he says we are learning how to change the environment, and that they have special means of using physical and biological technology to do so. What this means is they have learned to control perceptions and narratives. The media has become very adept at driving the narrative and creating perceptions that influence people to behave in certain ways. Look at Covid-19 for example. A well-crafted fear message, which according to Perloff[95] motivates people to act, can be effectively delivered and controlled through the major news outlets.

One of the best opportunities social scientists had to learn from people's reactions to media was The War of The Worlds radio broadcast in 1938. The presentation was masterfully done and drove many people across the country into a frenzied panic under the belief that America had been invaded by Martians. According to the book *Invasion from Mars: The Study of the Psychology of Panic,*[96] people were driven to such a state of fear that local water towers were shot by citizens who believed they were alien craft. Social scientists admitted that it was a rare opportunity to learn about how men react in stressful times while gaining valuable insight into his anxieties, intelligence, and social needs. Most of all, however, they learned that a radio broadcast was capable of driving men to react. Furthermore, they came to understand people had trust in the media and actors playing expert news broadcasters were instrumental in influencing behavior because of the publics inherent belief in authority figures.

Is it possible that today's media platform, a never-ending exhibition of talking heads telling us what to think, is based on what they learned about human behavior due to the War of the Worlds radio show? It is obvious that media is pushing persuasive messages designed to influence what we believe and how we behave. This will be discussed in greater detail later, so keep this information in mind. In the next chapter, we will look at the work of another social scientist who has taken the art of persuasive messaging to a new level in his attempts to influence and guide behavior.

Chapter Six
For our own good

A growing body of evidence demonstrates that behavioral science insights — research findings from fields such as behavioral economics and psychology about how people make decisions and act on them — can be used to design government policies to better serve the American people. (Barrack Obama Executive Order, September 2015)

In 2018 Time Magazine ran a piece called *The New Science of Happiness.*[97] The article is based on the new direction of psychology and the attempts to understand what it is that makes human beings happy. The field of positive psychology, like other behavioral sciences, is attempting to standardize, for a lack of a better word, what it means to live a satisfactory life. This is disturbing when you take into consideration the established approach that has already been set for studying such things by Skinner. This means that a study of happiness is being done from a secular, collective viewpoint that offers a one size fits all explanation.

The findings presented in Time Magazine's article seem to reflect Skinner's biases towards communal living and Utopianism. One of the first points they make represents the leftist, anti-capitalist view that the pursuit of wealth does not lead to a life of fulfillment and meaning. This is something we all understand. We do not need psychology to tell us money does not buy us joy. Their bigger point, when it comes to money, is that once an individual's basic needs are met, the pursuit of additional wealth does nothing to raise our happiness levels.

Who determines what constitutes our basic needs? Who decides what is best for us? Another finding they mentioned is the relationship between religion and happiness. Belonging to a religious community seems to contribute to feelings of happiness and belonging, but they are unclear if this is related to God, of just being part of a larger group.

For a science of happiness to exist then, these issues must be uniform and applicable to all people, in all situations. To suggest a one size fits all approach to being happy denies man of his individualism and his liberty to pursue that which makes him happy as a unique member of society. To create a scientific definition of happiness is to impose tyranny for your own good.

A science of human happiness could be serving a greater purpose. It is no coincidence that they are deliberately attempting to draw correlations between wealth and being happy. As the year 2021 kicks off, we are hearing more and more about something called The Great Reset.[98] This is being deemed as a start over of sorts, an opportunity created by the Covid-19 pandemic to reform global economics and the way human beings live their lives. For the real conspiracy theorists out there, the vision for the completion of this plan coincides with the established goals of the United Nations Sustainable Development Agenda.[99] Which by the way, is supposed to reach its desired end in the year 2030.

One of the slogans being used to promote this great reset builds off the anti-capitalist propaganda they have been feeding us for the past few decades. They claim we will own nothing and be happy about it. There is no doubt this belief is based on the studies they have done, but it is also likely they know what they have been teaching us for the past seventy years is having the desired effect. The whole point of this book up to this chapter has been to describe the conditioning that has brought Americans to a place where they will readily accept, if not demand, socialism.

When this Great Reset reaches its culmination, science will have attained its goal of redefining what it means to be human and, what it is we need to live more fulfilling lives. They will determine our needs and define our happiness. People will no longer feel the need to compete, there will be no more desire for wealth because our basic needs, as defined by them, will be provided by them.

Free markets and individualism are of course, a sickness that needs to be eradicated for man to reach his fullest potential. Capitalism, writes Jimmy Wu of Reason in Revolt,[100] is a system that leads to mass hopelessness, financial misery, despair and, higher rates of mental illness in any society. Religion has also long been viewed by many in psychology as inducive to mental illness. Marx went so far as to refer to it as the opiate of the masses.

Conservatism itself, as mentioned earlier, is thought to be a form of mental illness due to what the left refers to as a resistance to change. Given the fact that most conservatives believe in capitalism and religion, it is fair to say that those pursuing the science of happiness would feel our beliefs are making us miserable.

The science of happiness is attempting to heal the human soul based on the idea that capitalism keeps us trapped in an endless cycle of suffering and despair. They are attempting to create a new morality, as James Rachels discussed in *Created from Animals*, except they are building on what was already accomplished by the theory of evolution. They are instilling a system where they will rule over us with an iron fist and we will like it. This is of course, because the Utopian world they envision is better for everyone, in their minds. If only people would get rid of their old ideas and stop being so self-centered, we could perhaps, create such a world.

C.S. Lewis wrote in *The humanitarian theory of punishment,*[101] curing someone against their will for those ailments which are not real diseases is the same as being treated as animals or imbeciles. A tyranny of goodwill, he writes, is the most ruthless because the tyrant will oppress based on the belief, they are helping you. The only reason they would feel the need to create such a system is because they believe you need them to tell you how to live.

Cass Sunstein has taken the issue of influencing behavior for our own good to new heights. Co-author of the book *Nudge: Improving Decisions About Health, Wealth and Happiness*,[102] Sunstein, along with Richard Thaler, freely admit that they believe people are not capable of making decisions in their best interest. They need a "nudge" if they are expected to make good choices. Going back to Skinner briefly, he said they are learning how to change the environment to influence behavior through biological and technological means. Controlling our choices could certainly be considered influencing our environments. Social scientists, according to Sunstein and Thaler, have discovered through extensive research, there is a lack of rationality that goes into many of the decisions people make and, it is false to assume people will automatically make the best choices for themselves. This is a scary thought considering there is such a massive effort to control behavior and influence our opinions.

What Sunstein and Thaler are advocating for in *Nudge* is something called Libertarian Paternalism. This, according to Sunstein and Thaler, is the idea that people should be free to live their own lives and make their own choices. Sounds fair enough, right? Here is where it gets interesting. They claim that there is a legitimate role for what they refer to as *choice architects* to frame choices in a way that influences behavior for people's best interests.

They argue that the private sector and even government should act in ways that influence people to make better choices.

To be fair to Sunstein and Thaler, it is not being argued that they are in on some grand conspiracy to turn us all into good socialists. They openly state that it is not the intention of Libertarian Paternalism to cut people completely off from any behavior they freely choose to engage in, only to give them a nudge to change that behavior. In all honesty, it is not always a bad idea. Some people do behave in self-destructive ways. It is being suggested, however, that their understanding of how choices can be framed is being used in all levels of society to nudge people in certain directions. They openly say government can and should have a role in influencing opinion when it comes to issues of public policy. Like the environment and global warming and maybe gun control, for example.

There is a deceptive intonation to the whole idea of libertarian paternalism. While claiming to not infringe on people's freedom to choose for themselves, there is, at the same time, an admission that choice architecture requires the *elimination of choice*. This means that a choice architect is responsible for framing our choices in a way that presents the illusion of freedom but is offered in a way that encourages us to choose what they think is best for us. As an example, Sunstein and Thaler refer to a dinner party where the host purposely removes a bowl of nuts from the guests because if he does not, the guests will eat all the nuts and ruin their appetite. This assumes that the guests have no self-control and will automatically choose to engorge themselves on the nuts, with no thought of the potential consequences. While it is an innocent enough example, the question remains as to what degree such a technique of removing choices is being employed against the public.

On page 8 of *Nudge,* it is openly stated that many of society's biggest problems can be solved by "nudging" while insisting that people are freely making their own choices. The only problem is, you are freely choosing from controlled options meant to push you in one way or the other.

One of the best examples of this is something Sunstein and Thaler refer to as the default option. This is the framing of choice, where choosing the default, or, not going along with the other available choice, is seen as the path requiring the least effort. There is so much which goes into this from concepts and ideas that have been previously discussed. For instance, a default option is always likely to be chosen by people if it is presented in a way that suggests normality. We have already seen that people have a desire to fit in, so if the default is seen as the status quo most people will likely choose it. The best example of this is the issue of organ donation and the opt-in or opt-out options.[103]

When you get your driver's license, for example, you are asked if you would like to be an organ donor. Because you must explicitly choose to be an organ donor, with no opt-out option, very few people opt-in. Research shows when the default option is incorporated, and you must explicitly opt-out, leaving the opt-in as the default, organ donations increase. This is because very few people will take the time to look any further into the issue than just going along with the default under what Sunstein and Thaler refer to as the "yeah whatever" heuristic.

Basically, if the government or a large corporation wanted to push society in a certain direction, all that would be necessary is to frame their choices in a way that presents the desired behavior as the default option. As Sunstein and Thaler clearly say on page 83 of *Nudge,* a good choice architect has a very solid understanding of human behavior.

This concept is currently, or could be soon, being employed with the rollout of the Covid-19 vaccine. The *New England Journal of Medicine* ran a piece in the fall of 2020 discussing the idea that employers could be used to ensure people get vaccinated.[104] The whole premise behind the article was based on the knowledge that legally, a vaccine cannot be forced onto society. They argued because the public school system was successfully used to force parents to vaccinate their children, it is probable that employers could be used in the same way. Incentives and punishments could be used to persuade people into compliance with vaccine recommendations.

Several months after this article was published, The Washington Post ran a piece entitled *Employers prepare for coronavirus vaccine with a question: Can we require it?*[105] This has possibly been part of the plan all along as this article was published just two weeks before the vaccine was officially released with a massive propaganda campaign.

The interesting thing about this article is it discusses in a roundabout, deceptive kind of way, the use of the default option. If, for example, compliance with the vaccine could be presented as the default, or the normal course of action, people would likely comply. Another suggestion, which goes along with the knowledge people will generally take the path of least resistance, is employers make their people explain in a written statement why they are refusing to get the vaccine. Of course, this would only be effective if most people are complying, but it is based on the idea that people want to fit in. If they must explain why they are going against the grain with an unpopular position, they are more likely to just go along. This is not opinion, but an understanding of researched human behavior being employed for the purpose of persuading people into compliance with government objectives.

To what extent can government effectively frame our choices in a way that provides the illusion of freedom? It may seem like a ridiculous concept; however, they have dived into this subject more than the average person may realize. In 2015 when Sunstein was serving as President Obama's regulatory affairs Czar, Obama signed an executive order entitled *Using Behavioral Science Insights to Better Serve the American People*.[106] This is essentially an admission by the U.S. Government that everything we do is under the microscope. They are constantly studying our behavior from the perspective that we are little more than stimulus-response organisms, to figure out how to "nudge" us into going along while making it appear, we are freely choosing. Is it possible this could be employed with theories discussed earlier like fear-then-relief, to get us to choose the options government wants us to choose? The answer should be self-evident and concerning, considering the coming push for gun control.

Chapter Seven
The Role of the Media

The beauty of the system, however, is that such dissent and inconvenient information are within bounds and at the margins, so that while their presence shows that the system is not monolithic, they are not large enough to interfere unduly with the domination of the official agenda. (Herman & Chomsky, The Manufacturing of Consent: The Political economy of the Mass Media)

Imagine if the media, in collaboration with the government, could frame messages in a way which built off an understanding of human behavior and what likely course of action most people would take. In chapter 5, we saw that The War of the Worlds radio broadcast was an opportunity seized by social scientists to learn such things. In fact, Cantril specifically stated that this situation just might be the basic prototype, or model if you will, from which all future panics are studied.[107]

Cantril himself was instrumental in developing the use of propaganda through media. As a psychologist at Princeton University, he was affiliated with a Rockefeller-funded program studying the effects of radio broadcasts.[108] Rockefeller of course, is a name synonymous with the new world order conspiracy theories.

Cantril later went on to establish the Office of Public Opinion Research.[109] This organization studied the effectiveness of the United States' propaganda efforts through the Office of Strategic Services.[110] According to Alex Ansary, Cantril, with the help of Rockefeller money, helped develop a program known as the Princeton Listening Center with the explicit purpose of listening to Nazi brainwashing techniques and learning how to apply them to our own propaganda efforts. The Office of Strategic Services later became the Central Intelligence Agency.

The Princeton Listening Program paved the way for the United States Information Agency which according to Ansary, pushes propaganda for the National Security Council. Furthermore, Ansary also states that a key member of television media, Frank Stanton, was involved as well. He was an instrumental player in establishing Princeton's radio research program. He later became head of CBS's news broadcasting and sat as chairman of the board for The Rand Corporation.

According to a website called Media Bias Fact Check, The Rand Corporation is a think tank dedicated to problem-solving and helping communities around the world live safer, healthier and more prosperous lives.[111] Stanton was also a member of the Council on Foreign Relations, another organization known for pushing the U.S. into a global government.

People are growing increasingly suspicious of the mainstream media. For so long it was believed that there was a distinct split between the left and right when it came to news broadcasts. CNN and MSNBC for example, are considered extremely left-wing as they do little more than spew propaganda that reinforces the government-supported narrative. Fox News, on the other hand, has enjoyed the popular support of the conservative right as they have been viewed as being pro-America, and more importantly, Pro-Trump. That is until they called the election in favor of Biden in a way that conservatives considered to be too soon.[112]

Unfortunately, the perceived left-right paradigm between MSNBC, CNN, and Fox News is little more than an illusion. Fox News is owned by the Murdoch family and in July 2020, Rupert's son James and his wife donated 1.2 million dollars to the Biden campaign.[113] Furthermore, Rupert himself donated large sums of money to not only the Clinton's but to Chuck Schumer, Anthony Weiner, and John Kerry as well.[114]

While the perception of Fox News has been primarily a representation of the conservative view, the truth is their role has been to shape conservative belief. This is alluded to in Folkenflik's NPR article. He states that Fox News' role in shaping conservative thought was unrivaled in media. There is truth to this to a great degree. So-called conservatives from Fox News, along with other media talking heads, presented the Trump presidency as a brilliant strategy of four-dimensional chess. Every action Trump took was characterized as a carefully thought-out move which would eventually put the left in their place and drain the swamp. How does this reconcile with an owner of the network that has given so much money to the Democrats? Is there something else going on here?

In 2017, MSNBC's Mika Brzezinski took heat for saying, while on the air, that controlling what people think is the job of the media.[115] She attempted to walk this back of course. This statement was made during a conversation about President Trump controlling what his supporters believe. Apparently, she does not like competition.

The role of the media, to a large degree, is to control mass perception and the illusion of conflict between two parties largely pursuing the same political agenda. The idea of left and right-wing ideologies is a socially constructed perception designed to keep people trapped in their ways of thinking. As Folkenflik said, Fox News did not represent conservative thought as much as they *shaped* it.

Fox prides itself on being fair and balanced and has its fair share of liberal hosts who represent the other side. This is part of the deception. With the rest of the media being firmly in control of the left, the right was purposefully driven to Fox News, where there was still a fair share of liberal content. Fox News did not suddenly shift to the left as much as their intent was shifting the opinions of their viewers slightly to the left. Even though it was not one hundred percent successful. This claim is substantiated in a book called *Manufacturing of Consent: the political economy of the mass media.*[116]

Fox News, and the balanced approach they claim to take, is part of something called The Propaganda Model. According to Chomsky & Herman, this model of media deliberately allows for a small degree of dissention to present the illusion of autonomy. To make it appear as if the whole media apparatus is not controlled by the same two dozen or so corporations.[117] Questioning of the mainstream agenda, according to Chomsky & Sherman, is kept in check by the presence of those pushing the government-approved narrative. In other words, Fox News is the only mainstream outlet that lets the opposing side have such a large presence. The rest of the media is predominately liberal. The point is that the dissenting conservative views on Fox are presented in a narrow, controlled way with defined boundaries and enough opposition to keep it from growing and disrupting the real agenda.

Furthermore, to give some credibility to Folkenflik's comments on Fox News shaping conservative thought, Chomsky & Sherman state that the role of the media is to fix the ideologies taken for granted by the global elite, but likely rejected by the masses. This suggests that the role of the media is to do exactly as Brzezinski stated, tell us what we are supposed to think.

Conspiracy theorists are well familiar with the term "Operation Mockingbird."[118] This is the program where the CIA allegedly bought influence in the mainstream media while putting news broadcasters on the agency's payroll. According to Mary Louise, of Targtedjustice.net, the CIA had tens of thousands of operatives which had, by the late nineteen-fifties, infiltrated the nation's businesses, universities, and major media outlets. This program was started in the nineteen-forties by Frank Wisner, an undercover foreign service operative for the state department. [119]

Wisner recruited Washington Post publisher, Philip Graham, who was a graduate of the Army Intelligence school, to oversee Mockingbird. This establishes the connection between media and government interests. There are some interesting correlations to take note of. Louise stated in her article that the media presents a narrative which controls perceptions by defining opinions and the positions taken by the left and the right. The right-wing narrative is shaped by Fox news, for example, and the left, by CNN and other outlets.

Perhaps one of the most recognizable aspects of Mockingbird is the famous quote attributed to CIA director, William Casey. In a meeting with newly elected president Ronald Reagan in 1981, Casey was asked what his goals were as the new director. He allegedly replied by saying "we will know if our disinformation campaign is complete when everything the American people believe is false."[120]

Interestingly, there is no real evidence this was ever said. According to the website amallulla.org, it is attributed to a reporter who claims to have heard it firsthand while in the meeting. Her name was Barbara Honegger. Of course, if the CIA were involved in a massive disinformation campaign involving the media, this quote would have never been exposed in any media outlet. Some truths, however, speak for themselves. There is little doubt the media pushes a false narrative. The trick now is getting people to understand it is not just the liberal media that are in on it.

What exactly is the role of television media then? The War of the Worlds radio broadcast indicated that mass media can control behavior to a large degree based on the idea that people trust news broadcasters. News programs work from a carefully constructed fear message designed to encourage action for social change. As we discussed earlier, a good fear message not only strikes at the heart of viewers, but it also implies a recommended course of action to alleviate the fear or, solve the problem.

Earlier it was suggested the media works to present freedom itself as a dangerous concept. Something that threatens the safety and security of society. Interestingly, while the world is still living in fear over Covid-19, Dr. Fauci had some interesting things to say. He suggested that it is America's spirit of independence that prolonged the pandemic because too many people believed it is a hoax, failing to take the proper measures.[121] While this is Dr. Fauci saying this and not a major television network, it highlights the agenda of fear and discrediting American culture. America's freedom is responsible for suffering because people are not capable of being free, they need the government telling them what to do. As Suggested by Sunstein and Thaler's libertarian paternalism.

Covid-19 is one of the best examples of how the government, in collaboration with the media, works to control the narrative and define the parameters in which an argument can take place. In December 2020, Congress passed another Covid-19 relief stimulus bill totaling nine hundred billion dollars. American's would receive a six-hundred-dollar payment and, an additional three hundred dollars would be added onto unemployment benefits related to the coronavirus. President Trump sent this bill back to congress, but it was not because our government was spending billions on foreign aid. It was because the American worker was only getting six hundred dollars while billions were being sent overseas. At least, that is the perception.

President Trump demanded that the six hundred dollars be increased to two thousand per person. While this seems like a noble thing to do, making Trump supporters believe he is fighting for them, the argument was framed from the perspective that socialism is the only solution. Opening the economy and ending the restrictions that forced so many to close their businesses and lose their livelihoods is not even part of the equation. Looking into the controversial data that brings the whole Covid-19 narrative into question is not even part of the conversation.

By presenting the issue as a Trump vs. the left argument, they have successfully brought a large portion of the population to support policies, and behave in ways they may not have otherwise, by making them demand more government spending. Handing out two thousand dollars in stimulus, when we are already twenty-seven trillion in debt, is indeed socialism whether people realize it or not.

According to Vox magazine, seventy-four percent of potential voters agreed that increasing spending was more important than reigning in the national debt.[122] As it stands right now, the national debt breaks down to roughly seventy-one thousand dollars per American. It has been speculated that Trump's last stimulus bill, with six-hundred-dollar payouts, would increase this amount by roughly six thousand dollars. If the amount is kicked up to two thousand, this would rise astronomically.

The ironic thing that most Americans would not even notice is that the two thousand dollars Trump is demanding is the same amount Democrats want for their Universal Basic Income scheme. In April 2020, shortly after the first Covid-19 stimulus bill was passed, the Democrats introduced H.R. 6496, The Emergency Money for the People Act[123] which calls for direct payments of two thousand dollars per American throughout the Covid-19 pandemic. The idea of a universal basic income has been discussed for some time but the problem for them is getting it accomplished with the approval of the American people.

According to an article at Bizpacreview.com[124] Nancy Pelosi allegedly tweeted something suggesting that they finally got Trump to agree to the two-thousand-dollar amount. This suggests one of two things, either President Trump is easily manipulated, or he is just playing along. In any case, the point is the way this issue was framed, people were persuaded or tricked into accepting socialism. The elements of fear and desperation played their role in guiding the thinking of Americans and getting them to, as Alinsky says, forget the past and chance the future. To accept the change they may not otherwise, while behaving in a manner they normally would not. It was presented within the framework of the Hegelian Dialectic. The problem was too much money going overseas and not enough for Americans. The demand was to increase how much Americans would get, which, it just so happens, was the pre-determined solution. The latest news at the time of this writing was that Senate Republicans were working to block the increased payments to Americans. This of course, would do little more than further fracture the republican base, while reinforcing support for Trump. (Of course, in March 2021, President Biden signed another stimulus bill handing out $1400 to Americans.)

There is another interesting example concerning Covid-19 that deserves mentioning because it also highlights how the media can shape a narrative, which in turn, guides thoughts and opinions. This is the development of the Covid vaccine which became available in early December 2020. Throughout the so-called Covid pandemic, many of Trump's biggest supporters held on to the idea that the virus was deliberately created to destroy Trump's booming economy. Little attention was being paid to the fact that Trump pushed some of the guidelines which led to the damaging shutdowns in the first place.[125]

In April 2020, Donald trump allegedly pulled funding from the World Health Organization due to its misleading representation of coronavirus data. Interestingly, the story was framed from the perspective that people like Bill Gates opposed such a move.[126] This narrative reinforces support for Trump because he is seen as taking a stand when on the other hand, he quietly donated over a billion dollars to the Gates vaccine alliance, striking a deal with Pfizer for a Covid vaccine.[127] The socially constructed conflict presents the illusion that Trump is standing against the forces of evil while he is simultaneously funding them.

After the election, an interesting story popped up depicting a conflict between New York Governor Andrew Cuomo and President Trump concerning the vaccine. Andrew Cuomo is a vile, anti-American leftist who incidentally, received thousands of dollars in political donations from Donald Trump.[128] Cuomo accused Trump of bragging about his vaccine progress because he is upset about losing the election. What Cuomo said is that Trump is fast- tracking the vaccine to get one approved before leaving office. You know, so he can take the credit.[129] Trump responded in kind by saying that New York would not be receiving the vaccine. By the way, Trump should indeed, take all the credit.

Again, this narrative reinforces the idea that there is a fierce conflict occurring between the left and right when truthfully, this constructed conflict is designed to reinforce support for an agenda. Conservatives are now hailing the development of the Covid vaccine as one of Trump's greatest accomplishments. The question of whether we even need a vaccine when the survival rate for Covid is 98.6% has vanished from the conversation altogether. They have successfully framed the argument so that we are arguing it from the perspective that we need the vaccine.

Americans have been exposed to continuous chaos and trauma since at least, the September 11, 2001 terror attacks. The media, since that time, has been used to create a state of mind that is always reacting to a frightening stimulus. Constant shootings, economic problems, global warming, war, terrorism, and of course, killer viruses by the dozens. Zika, mrsa, sars, bird flu, swine flu, and Ebola, to name just a few in the past ten years alone. Even as this chapter was being written, Dr. Fauci was warning Americans of a new, more infectious strain of Covid-19 that threatens to wipe us all out if we do not surrender our lives to the government.[130]

All of this is being done with a keen understanding of how fear affects the psyche. It could be theoretically argued that America is in a constant state of post-traumatic stress. According to an article in the *Journal of Behavior Therapy and Experimental Psychiatry*,[131] traumatic memories can be triggered when the brain receives a stimulus in the context of that traumatic event. It does not have to be the same, nor does it have to have a meaningful relationship with the original trauma.

This is of course, the standard definition of post-traumatic stress disorder. Given the evidence presented in this chapter, it must be considered that media, along with the government and other powers that be, are deliberately creating panic to guide and further learn how to predict your behavior. When we see a mass shooting for example, and they call it home grown terrorism, with terrorism being the keyword, our brains are subconsciously reminding us of the horror of September 11 because of the association with the word terrorism. Furthermore, with every mass shooting that occurs, our reactions to anything gun-related are likely to be the same due to the created association between the second amendment and mass murder.

Associationism is a theory of learning which posits the idea that learning occurs, and behaviors are shaped, based on an individual's history which may be related to whatever event is taking place.[132] It must be considered that those behind the scenes, creating the media narrative, understand that they can shape behavior by keeping people in a state of fear to one degree or another. In the next chapter, we will dive a little deeper into the theories of fear messages, propaganda, and some of the models used to examine behavior motivated by fear.

Chapter Eight
Fear appeals and Covid-19

Devising an effective fear appeal, is to some extent, an art, but it is an art that requires a scientist's appreciation of the intricacies of human behavior. (Perloff, Dynamics of Persuasion: Communication and Attitudes in the 21st Century)

The larger point of this book thus far has been to show that there is a deliberate effort to change the perceptions and attitudes of the American people, making them more likely to accept change they may not otherwise. We have looked briefly into the use of critical theory, Skinner's science of behavior, prescription drugs and, the media's role in shaping popular thought. We also looked at Cass Sunstein's libertarian paternalism and how our choices can be manipulated. Finally, the issue of well-crafted fear messages was also discussed. All these topics are well deserving of independent study and much has been written about them. Their mention in this book was intended to show a relationship in how they have been used to create a society that favors big government collectivism over personal liberty.

It is one thing to suggest we are being propagandized by the media, or the public education system is brainwashing our children. There is a science to it, a methodology if you will which is based largely on what they know about human behavior. To take the view that human beings have no independent will of their own, as most behaviorists do, is misleading and a view they simply do not believe in themselves. If it were true, there would be no need to study our behavior to such an extent as to find ways to induce compliance with their agendas.

Even Skinner admits that often, the goal is to change behavior and not a person's belief because people have a tremendous ability to resist. Behavior change is often due to a shift in environmental circumstances which forces the individual to change the way they act. What does it matter if the person retains their beliefs if they are falling in line and not acting on them? One of those environmental factors is of course, fear. In this chapter, we will dive deeper into its use and the models from which fear-based behaviors are examined.

According to a study entitled *Appealing to fear: A meta-analysis of fear appeal effectiveness and theories,*[133] fear messages are most effective when presented with an efficacy statement and the perception of being highly vulnerable to the perceived danger. An efficacy statement is the suggestion of a desired course of action, which is said to alleviate the threat. If the threat is presented along with a solution, it is more likely to affect behavior in the desired way. This makes sense because looking back to Chapter One, we saw what Perloff[134] described as the *fear-then relief* technique. He stated the feeling of relief associated with the presented solution is conducive to attitude change. This is because the feeling of being relieved produces a mindless state where one is less likely to ask any questions if they know they no longer face the alleged danger.[135]

This study also claims to answer whether the use of fear appeals can backfire. This has been somewhat controversial, with many scholarly articles claiming they do. According to Perloff, fear appeals can backfire if it pushes an individual too far into what is referred to as fear control, opposed to danger control. Fear control is when in an individual is acting to keep his fear at bay, which is not the desired behavior a fear message is supposed to induce. An effective appeal motivates one to act to alleviate the danger, requiring the desired behavioral change.

There is no better example of a fear appeal than the messaging driving the Covid-19 agenda. The appeal is getting ill from a new, unknown virus, and the recommended course of action is total compliance with government dictates. This has been highly effective due to a constant stream of never-ending propaganda depicting Covid-19 as a global pandemic.

Interestingly, fear messages are most effective when presented with a singular behavioral adjustment as opposed to repeated behaviors.[136] Mask wearing, and economic shutdowns cannot be considered changes that occur only once but are extreme courses of action requiring dedication. This will be discussed in greater detail soon. The overall findings of this study show that fear appeals are remarkably effective in influencing behavioral and attitude changes.

There was a different approach taken by the authors of this study that examined the effects of fear messages in their totality. Typically, one of three theoretical approaches is taken when examining the effects fear has on behavior. These are message content, recommended behavioral change, and the intended audience.[137] This study included all three in their analysis to gain a better understanding of how fear influences one to act. It is reasonable to conclude that viewing an individual's motivation to act through the lens of only one of these approaches would be limited in scope. This is the problem of scientific studies. They are almost always based on a model which defines the boundaries in which the study can take place. When it comes to studies concerning human behavior, they too are based on models. Models mind you, that fall within the parameters of an established science of human behavior.

There are several models of behavior from which fear appeals are studied. The drive reduction model, the parallel process model, the extended parallel process model, the protection motivation theory, the situational theory of publics, and last but certainly not least, the U.S. public health service belief model,[138] also known simply as the health belief model. The HBM will be examined more deeply than the others for obvious reasons. The year 2020 will always be remembered because of the Covid-19 pandemic and the damage it wrought. Most of this was due to the perceived danger of a new killer virus where many people simply went along with the news being presented, without doing any substantial research for themselves.

The drive reduction model, according to Williams, views fear as a state of mind putting one into a "drive mode" motivated by the need to alleviate the discomfort. Interestingly, there are some correlations to the fear-then-relief ideas. This model assumes that following the recommended course of action produces a reinforcing sense of relief. It also suggests that a fear message that produces little arousal is not enough to motivate behavioral change. The message must be almost, panic-inducing. Perloff[139] notes that there must be an illusion of vulnerability present. If a person does not feel threatened, why would they follow along with recommended behavioral changes?

The parallel and extended parallel process models are based on the idea that if pushed too hard, the fear appeal may not provoke the desired reaction. This was discussed earlier with fear control vs. danger control. Taking action to avoid danger is generally what the fear appeal is designed to do. People can control the emotion of fear without making any drastic behavioral changes. To avoid physical danger, however, requires making changes based on environmental factors. If the environment presents a dangerous situation, people will have to make changes of some kind to avoid it. The *extended parallel process* model looks at fear as something that causes one to reject the message altogether and it is the efficacy message or a promise of solutions, that really motivates attitude change.

Protection motivation theory works from the knowledge that people will take meaningful action and are motivated to protect themselves from perceived dangers. The model is based on two cognitive processes, the perception of the threat and their ability to implement the recommended changes.[140] One of the considerations taken when deciding a course of action under this theory, and because it's scientific, it is not referred to as a choice, rather a response to a stimulus, is the probability of the threat occurring if no action is taken. This theory is a good example of how behavioral models are limited in their scope because there is not anything new here. People will always take action to avoid danger, we would not be human if we did not. Under this theory, it is through the narrowly defined borders of a theoretical approach which motivates people to take action to protect themselves from danger. The parameters are defined and controlled by those that developed the theory. If a study is being done under this model, or any of the other ones for that matter, it is being done in a way that forces the behavior to fit the theory.

The situational theory of publics is a different approach altogether. It examines different populations that face similar problems, and the differences in how they react to fear-based messages. It differentiates between those that can be viewed as responding to the threat and those that do nothing[141] by breaking people down into three categories of responsiveness. Those who have no problem recognition and as a result, no involvement. Those who have high problem recognition and still no involvement and finally, those who have both high problem recognition and high levels of involvement.[142] This is an interesting perspective because it suggests that to some degree, those crafting a message for a particular population may already have a good idea of how these categories break down.

For example, this model may be used to assess a city's population to ascertain their susceptibility to a message and, their willingness to comply. This is interesting considering all the cities currently enforcing mask mandates and lockdowns.

The existence of so many models from which fear can be studied is a prime example of what is wrong with studying human behavior from a scientific perspective. There is no room for individuality and all behavior must be, for the sake of obtaining consistent results, standardized. This is what Skinner meant in *Science and Human Behavior*. Truthfully, there is not much of a difference between these theories at all. They all work from the premise that fear is motivating an individual to take an action of some kind to alleviate it. Fear itself is an uncomfortable emotion, of course people will seek ways to rid themselves of it. To make a science of behavior out of it, to determine how susceptible people are to persuasion is downright wicked. There may be times when an effective appeal to fear may be warranted if it is truly meant to change behavior for the better. After all, advertising campaigns aimed at getting people to quit smoking are based on fear appeals. They can be considered fallacious, however, if used to influence behaviors without sufficient evidence justifying it.[143]

This brings us to the model which bears the most relevance to what we are experiencing today, *The Health Belief Model.* Looking at things from the perspective of the Covid-19 pandemic, it could be argued this model expands on the visions of Hadley Cantril when he said the War of the Worlds study could be the prototype for future studies of panic. The Health Belief model ties all the essential elements together. In fact, there has already been studies concerning Covid-19 based on The Health Belief Model that will be examined thoroughly from here on out. First though, a brief explanation of the model itself.

The Health Belief Model, according to an article from JMIR Public Health and Surveillance,[144] is a model used to understand health-related choices. Behaviors are predicted in much the same way as other models. The desire to avoid a threat and the effectiveness of the offered solution are the main mediums in which certain actions are predicted. The model itself approaches the issue of behavioral choices both from Skinner's view of stimulus-response and, a cognitive perspective.[145] This means it is believed the benefits of taking appropriate actions to avoid illness will reinforce correct behavior from the former, while the latter suggests people are actively choosing which course of action is best based on perceived expectations. In other words, the Health Belief Model has been used to examine behaviors from both a stimulus-response and cognitive theory approach.

There are four main theoretical approaches that are believed to motivate human behavior when it comes to health-related threats. Take note of the keyword in each of these approaches. *Perceived* susceptibility, *perceived* severity, *perceived* barriers and, *perceived* benefits.[146] The word perceived of course, relates to how the health threat is viewed by either the individual or society. Susceptibility refers to a person's fear of their own vulnerability. Severity of course refers to the seriousness of the threat. The perceived benefits relate to the belief in the recommended course of action and the perceived barriers refer to the psychological costs of following such recommendations.

A good example of a perceived barrier, from the perspective of someone using the model to conduct a study, would be facemasks. Despite mandates, many people refuse to wear a mask everywhere they go because it comes with a cost. There is no science that suggests forcing healthy people to wear masks has any effect on anything. There is a perception that will be discussed later. Another good example is the Covid-19 vaccine. People's refusal to get vaccinated would be considered a barrier because of the negative associations with the recommended course of action, prompting people to not follow along.

The most important point to consider when it comes to the keyword perceived is the source of the perception. In Cantril's War of the Worlds study, if you remember, it was learned that people largely believed what they were hearing because of the trust they placed in media figures. According to the JMIR article, the media plays a crucial role in shaping the constructs of the Health Belief Model. News reports, along with government policies and recommendations, are considered *cues to action,* which are believed to motivate people's behavior. The media then, shapes and controls the perceptions of the public. If the government wanted to force economic shutdowns and mask mandates, or even vaccines, then it makes sense that the media would be responsible for pushing the fear message meant to alter behavior. At the time of this writing, (January 1st) the vaccine was being slowly released to the public while news stories were being released describing a new strain of Covid-19 hitting American shores.

Again, it may not be morally wrong to use a well-crafted fear message to encourage behavior that may save someone's life. To push agendas which go against the basic principles of liberty and justice, however, is altogether different. Covid-19 could undoubtedly be considered an example of a fear appeal that has no evidence to justify the government mandates, making it a fallacious use of fear appeals.[147] Covid-19 has been nothing but contradictions and controversy since the pandemic first started back in the winter of 2020. If you think about it, the rolling out of the crisis was brilliantly planned. It started with frightening images of Chinese health workers donned in full hazmat gear spraying down buildings and ripping people out of their homes. By the time it reached American shores people were already deathly afraid, making them more susceptible to government recommendations. The only problem is that Covid-19 is not any more deadly than a seasonal flu with a 0.26% fatality rate, as admitted by the CDC.[148]

There has been so much misleading and confusing information that any sane country would have put an end to the harmful lockdowns and mask mandates. Even Dr. Fauci, in an article he penned in *The New England Journal of Medicine* in March 2020 admitted that Covid-19 had a case fatality rate of less than one percent.[149] Of course, this assessment assumes that asymptomatic cases are higher, and more people than earlier realized, had already been infected.

Ten months later nothing much has changed, Covid-19 still has an incredibly low fatality rate. Despite having admitted this, Fauci has come to be known as a master of propaganda as he takes to the air regularly to push his fear porn. Over the course of the last year, we have seen the CDC admit that hospitals had a financial incentive to label all deaths as Covid-19, if possible.[150] As recent as September 2020, the CDC admitted that 94% percent of covid-19 deaths were related to other life-threatening medical conditions.[151] This means people were dying with

Covid, not from Covid. This story was reported by the mainstream media and it should have been enough to put an end to the whole thing altogether. Unfortunately, people are not paying attention. This lack of attentiveness is something they surely took note of.

We must go back to something that Cass Sunstein and Richard Thaler said in *Nudge,*[152] that was mentioned in Chapter one. People lack the cognitive ability to see how their opinion may change if a problem was presented differently. Here we have a mainstream media source virtually admitting that Covid-19 is not the world-ending killer pandemic people thought it was, and no one said anything. An updated report was released by the CDC on January 14, 2021, where the numbers reflecting Covid deaths were once again, readjusted. Furthermore, the report admitted that often, a person can be diagnosed with Covid-19 with or without verifiable confirmation from a laboratory.

> "COVID-19 deaths are identified using a new ICD–10 code. When COVID-19 is reported as a cause of death — or when it is listed as a "probable" or "presumed" cause — the death is coded as U07.1. This can include cases with or without laboratory confirmation."[153]

You must wonder if contradicting information is deliberately put out there simply to see how the public reacts to it. It is entirely possible that conclusions such as Sunstein and Thaler's are reached because they are gauging the public reactions to media stories which purposefully present the lie in one way, and the truth in another.

Perhaps the biggest and most controversial contradiction is the existence of the virus itself. After a year of hearing blatant inconsistencies and news about false positive PCR test results, the World Health Organization finally admitted that the testing process is flawed.[154]

> "That PCR tests have exceptionally high false result rates is something that experts have already been warning the public of, even in the early days of the COVID-19 pandemic. The higher the cycle threshold (CT), i.e., the number of amplification cycles used to detect RNA particles, the greater the chances of a false positive. Yet the CDC still recommends running PCR tests at a CT of 40 — even though anything over 35 should be deemed scientifically unjustifiable." (Mercola)

This is primarily because the CDC has readily admitted in their own document that a purified, isolated sample of the virus was not available to them when the test was developed.[155]

> "Since no quantified virus isolates of the 2019-nCoV were available for CDC use at the time the

test was developed and this study conducted, assays designed for detection of the 2019-nCoV RNA were tested with characterized stocks of in vitro transcribed full-length RNA." (CDC)

Of course, this statement was fact-checked when reported through other media outlets and claimed to be false because of a misrepresentation of the science, however, there must be an answer as to why there are so many false positives. Simply saying the science was taken out of context does not produce an isolated, purified virus. According to Dr. Kevin Corbett,[156] evidence of a new disease must be published before being revealed as such. Furthermore, Corbett states that virus purification is an absolute must when developing tests if the gold standard in test manufacturing is to be met.

> "There is no gold standard for COVID-19 since this specific virus has never been properly purified and visualized. Thus, the accuracies of the tests are unknown. The development of these test kits is contrary to the FDA's guidance document." (Kevin Corbett)

The fact no purified virus was available during the development of the test was all but admitted, as shown, by the CDC. This explains the false positives being so high and is another contentious reality which should have motivated the public to demand an end to any restrictions or other mandates associated with Covid-19. The people, however, have been largely silent and compliant with the government's orders. We know that this is because there are inconsistencies between what people have come to believe and information that goes against those beliefs. Again, it should be considered, based on the very topic and information provided in this book, that they deliberately feed us misinformation to study our behavior to better determine how to guide our thinking. In the following chapter we will dive into the Health Belief Model and the two existing studies which have had tremendous influence on how the message has been crafted to induce compliance with Covid-19 objectives.

Chapter Nine
The Facemask Study

We found that individuals are more likely to wear facemasks due to the *perceived* susceptibility and *perceived* severity of being afflicted with life-threatening diseases. Although *perceived* susceptibility appeared to be the most significant factor determining compliance, *perceived* benefits of mask-wearing was found to have significant effects on mask-wearing compliance as well. (Singapore Medical Journal)

In 2014, the Singapore Medical Journal published a study entitled *The use of facemasks to prevent respiratory infection: A literature review in the context of the Health Belief Model.*[157] The article makes the initial claim facemasks have, in the past, been proven to prevent respiratory infections. It concluded by saying further studies are needed to determine the effectiveness of such interventions. What interventions are they talking about? The use of facemasks or something else?

There is no science showing that facemasks prevent people from getting sick. The most you might find is that their use by a sick person may limit the spread of infected aerosol particles. The latest study[158] determined that there is no significant difference at all between infection rates of those who wear masks and those who do not.

Another study attempting to ascertain the effectiveness of facemasks was published by the National Library of Medicine.[159] In other words, this was a government study. It concluded that medical and cloth masks, in a health care environment, were ineffective at preventing flu-like illnesses while respirators offered more protection for healthcare workers. The article suggested that the use of facemasks could be effective, if worn by sick people, in preventing the infection of healthy people. The problem with this study is it was conducted in a health care setting. It is reasonable to conclude that in a controlled environment, mask use by sick people could limit the spread of infection.

The suggestion that mask use by healthy people prevents infection assumes that asymptomatic carriers are potentially spreading the disease. The World Health Organization stated in June 2020[160] that asymptomatic spread is rare, while America's media continues to suggest it is primarily responsible for most cases.[161] In fact, a recent study evaluating millions of people determined that asymptomatic transmissions simply do not occur.[162]

The idea suggesting people with no symptoms can spread sickness is the big lie that is convincing people to wear masks. Technically, they can say there is scientific evidence suggesting mask use works, however, it is most effective in preventing sick people from spreading infection. If they can convince the population that they may be asymptomatic carriers, they can potentially convince them to wear masks.

Going back to the study conducted by the Singapore Medical Journal, the interventions they are discussing are the methods used in persuading people to cover their own face. The authors specifically state that complex interventions based on the health belief model, such as perceived susceptibility and severity, are needed to increase community facemask use. In other words, the big lie that asymptomatic people are most responsible for spreading Covid-19 is being used as a tool of persuasion to get people to comply. They are using fear and mistrust to nudge people into compliance with their objectives.

Before getting into the main point of this chapter, it is important to understand some limitations of the Health Belief Model.[163] As mentioned in the last chapter, much of this model is based on stimulus-response theory. Meaning that people are simply responding to cues they are being fed without giving too much thought to what they are doing. This is a huge limitation because it assumes people are mindless and unable to make their own behavioral choices.

The Health Belief model does not account for individuality, which as pointed out earlier, is a problem with all models of human behavior. Perhaps the most interesting assumption is the idea that so-called *"cues to action,"* are effective in getting people to act, and that a person's health is the primary factor in decision making. In other words, it assumes that a fear message targeting health-related behavior will be effective because we are unable to think on our own.

Cues to action[164] are defined as the stimulus needed to push one into performing the desired behavior. They could be physical symptoms or, a media campaign constantly pushing the information needed. In fact, this was a determining factor in the Singapore Medical Journal study.

> "Media blitz and public health promotion activities supported by government agencies provide cues to increase the public's usage of facemasks." (Singapore Medical Journal)

Getting people to comply with mask mandates can be described as an absolute work of evil genius. Somewhere, someone is rubbing their hands together and twirling the end of their curved mustache, anxious to see what else they can get us to comply with. Using the pretext of asymptomatic carriers, they worked off a common trait of human behavior, knowing that people can be easily controlled by their own efforts.

Returning to the theory of effort justification, B.F. Skinner said in *Beyond Freedom and Dignity* that people who "work productively because of the reinforcing value of what they produce are under the sensitive and powerful control of the products."[165] This is the same thing as virtue signaling. The wearing of a mask in the name of protecting others has become a virtue that people are now controlled by. They are living under the illusion that they somehow have a higher sense of morality than those who refuse to wear masks.

Effort justification is a by-product of cognitive dissonance. It is a way of alleviating tension resulting from conflicting beliefs and actions.[166] People tend to put a lot of effort into anything they may deem to be a worthy cause. In fact, this effort has shown to be instrumental in changing attitudes towards the achievement of the goal associated with the effort. In the case of mask wearing there was a dissonance, a conflict between what they knew was wrong and the feeling that it might be for the greater good. Because the media constantly displayed the lie of asymptomatic carriers, people viewed it as a worthy cause. Now, just as the theory suggests, their attitudes towards mask-wearing have changed because of their beliefs in the effort they are putting into it. People will put more value into a goal that requires greater effort to achieve. Wearing a mask every day under the belief that you are protecting others, even though you are not sick, requires great effort.

The wearing of masks has become a virtue signal of sorts. A sign of moral superiority of the wearer that shows they care about you and are willing to sacrifice their own freedom for your safety. It is a way of solidifying a vision you want others to have of yourself.[167] It is more about wanting to appear as a good person, or a doer of good deeds, opposed to doing them. Virtue signaling in this sense, is not a good thing if the signal overrides any sense of a real value.

What you end up with, in many cases, is accusatory attitudes on both sides of the issue. On one side is the attitude being displayed by the signaler suggesting there is a moral superiority and, failing to fall in line, demonstrates a lack of compassion. On the other side, is the accusation someone is merely hiding behind an issue to make themselves look and or, feel good.

In the case of mask-wearing, those complying think the non-maskers lack compassion for others, and those refusing to wear masks look at those wearing them as sheep. An interesting op-ed entitled *The psychological manipulation of universal masking*[168] draws some correlations between the propaganda being used today and that of Nazi Germany. The repetitive use of popular slogans which appeal to emotional virtue, for example, and presenting the issue from a morally superior viewpoint as another. The tactic of using words like anti-masker and presenting those that refuse to wear masks as selfish and uncaring are effective in pressuring others into compliance. This is causing a major divide in society. None of this is to say that everyone wearing a mask, or refusing to do so, falls in line with these descriptions. Some people wear them because their job dictates it.

The next study revolved around the use of social media to gauge people's opinions towards other Covid-19 policies, like social distancing. *The Use of the Health Belief Model-based deep learning classifiers for Covid-19 social media content to examine public perceptions of physical distancing,*[169] examines the public attitudes towards intervention policies through the lens of the Health Belief Model. The purpose is to better understand effective ways to form effective policy recommendations. It's funny how that word perception keeps coming up under the use of this model, isn't it?

The methodology of this study revolves around gauging the comments made on social media in response to existing policies put forth by public health entities like CDC and Public Health England. The comments were categorized in relation to the four major perspectives of the HBM: perceived susceptibility, severity, barriers, and benefits. Messages from media and government were aimed at altering personal behavior patterns in relation to the perceptions the public held on Covid-19 interventions. The study's biggest objective was to develop models of studying the public's reactions to these messages that could be used to quickly analyze the public's perceptions, using what they referred to as "deep-learning text classification."

In other words, this is a data mining operation and the public's opinions are helping those responsible for framing the message do so more effectively. They are studying your behavior and learning how to manipulate it in real-time. The study concludes by saying they fully intend to conduct future studies pertaining to facemasks as well.

The point of this chapter is that the studies examined were not done to prove the efficacy of mask-wearing or other interventions but to find ways to induce compliance with recommended mandates. To devote so much effort into getting people to go against their own common sense implies a deception of sorts.

Truth is self-evident, and when it comes to Covid-19, it is obvious to many people that we are being lied to. If the disease were as deadly as they would like us to believe, there would be no need to manipulate our behavior. People would willingly adopt the necessary behavior changes simply based on what they can see for themselves. What people are seeing is propaganda and, an attempt to keep us in a state of fear.

The biggest mistake on the part of social science is viewing human behavior from the Darwinist perspective. It is all too apparent that they themselves do not believe that people are so gullible and stupid. If we were, there would not be a whole science dedicated to studying and manipulating our behavior to meet their ends. In the best-case scenario, the study of behavior from a Darwinist perspective has tied the hands of science while contributing to the development of models that do not account for human free will. In the worst case, it is a deliberate attempt to guide us towards an end we would otherwise reject.

What is the purpose of mask mandates then? Andy Andrews, in his remarkable eighty-page book, *How Do You Kill 11 Million People?*[170] asks a simple question. How did the Jewish people of Nazi Germany allow themselves to be so mercilessly rounded up and murdered? The answer of course, is that they fell for the big deception.

Andrews describes this as an intricate set of lies, designed explicitly to subdue the consciousness of the Jews by appealing to their needs and desires. It started by placing barricades around Jewish neighborhoods in the name of safety. The lie suggesting every infringement against their freedom was for their safety was repeated endlessly, to the point of them willingly getting on the trains when they were told the Russians were coming. There was little that could be done, even by those who questioned what was going on because mass compliance empowered the machine. If you questioned why there was a need for barricades you were ridiculed into silence because you did not care for the safety of your neighbors.

The big intricate lie here, as mentioned earlier, is the idea that we are wearing masks to prevent the asymptomatic spread of a disease that has not been isolated and purified. Studies were done and conclusions were reached based on the perceptions the public had concerning the disease and the mandated interventions. Perceptions which were no doubt, shaped by media and others skilled in the art of crafting an effective message. The result is a population that is largely complying without question, despite the contradictions in the evidence. Remember earlier, when it was revealed that those involved in Operation Mockingbird were involved in a project called the Princeton Listening Center? This was an operation dedicated to studying Nazi propaganda for the *purpose of applying it to our own media efforts.*

After World War Two, many German scientists were brought to the United States under the operational name of Operation Paperclip.[171] This of course, is where our space program took a flying leap with the invention of the V-2 rocket. According to an article at History.com, Harry Truman prohibited the recruitment of known Nazi's and war criminals into the program however, the Office of Strategic Services scrubbed the records of many of the people brought into our country. The Office of Strategic Services was also mentioned earlier as being involved in propaganda efforts. If we were bringing in German Scientists, while also being involved in programs that studied their compliance gaining methods, it seems reasonable to conclude that we brought their social scientists over as well.

In other words, it is highly likely, though speculative, that what is known about compliance gaining pertaining to mask use, comes directly from the methods used to get the Jews to willingly comply with their own demise. Looking at things from this perspective really begs the question as to why they are pushing mask mandates so hard. What are they really trying to achieve? To merely say control is a massive understatement. They already have a fair amount of control over the population looking at how many people are complying.

What they are doing is learning, and by complying without question, you are teaching them. In the coming months, with Biden as president, we will no doubt be facing massive efforts to pass gun control legislation. This will be accompanied by media campaigns designed to discredit and demonize gun owners. Just what reason does the government have to believe that they cannot get us to comply in one way or the other? Yes, the mandates are about control, but they are also massive studies in compliance, and they are keenly watching how the population responds or fails to respond, to every bit of information they feed us. We are after all, in the eyes of the communists, nothing but a stimulus-response animal.

"Having no independent will of his own, man is easily handled by stimulus-response mechanisms. It is only necessary to install a stimulus into the mental anatomy of man to have that stimulus reactivate and respond anytime an exterior command source calls it into being". (Brainwashing: A Synthesis on the Russian Textbook of psychopolitics.)[172]

Chapter Ten
Final Thoughts

I realized then just what Khrushchev meant when he said the United States would be defeated without a shot being fired. This experience motivated me to find answers on my own. Writing then, became the means in which I educated myself.

This was hardly an all-encompassing book. There are many aspects of change which were not included while, any one of the topics which were discussed, are worthy of books all their own. The point was to show the reader there is much more than meets the eye and the problem is much more complex than framing it from a Republican vs. Democrat perspective.

These are words which in all truth, we no longer define on our own terms. For instance, Webster's dictionary now defines fascism as a right-wing phenomenon. Whenever someone seeks a definition of that word, the idea that it is a right-wing ideology will be forever impressed in their consciousness. As a political ideology, fascism may be to the right of communism, but it is far left of center when it comes to human freedom.

This book was written because I have come to see change requires action. The left has mastered the skills of understanding human behavior and they have rallied their troops to a cause they are committed too. They have changed the very fabric of this nation in a stealthy, almost silent manner going unnoticed by most people.

On the other hand, Republicans have lived their lives in a very live and let live fashion. Going to work every day, raising their families, paying their taxes. Blissfully unaware that people could hate the idea of freedom so much, they would go to the lengths they have to destroy it.

While the conservative right has certainly awakened to the danger, it is far too little and too late to make any meaningful attempts to stop the fundamental transformation choo-choo train. The reason is because Republicans largely misunderstand the nature of the left, the beliefs they hold, and the methodologies they employ. To the average Republican voter, it is difficult to understand why anyone would want to change this country, let alone the idea that our behaviors are constantly being studied to be used against us.

Republicans have traditionally believed in the principles which originally defined this nation; therefore, wrapping their head around the idea that someone would deliberately attempt to destroy their own freedom is difficult.

Some may argue that writing a book is hardly taking action that could affect meaningful change. This is true, but to me, this is more than a book. This is a culmination of my own understanding, based on an experience I had that demanded answers. As mentioned earlier, while a student in a social work program I was told I was not fit for the profession because of my opposition to concepts like white privilege and social justice. I realized then just what Khrushchev meant when he said the United States would be defeated without a shot being fired. This experience motivated me to find answers on my own. Writing then, became the means in which I educated myself.

The more I learned, the more I dedicated myself to educating others. There is a process in writing one goes through where the writer is initially writing to gain knowledge about a particular topic and, the work itself is done for the writer's own benefit. Gradually, the subject becomes more focused and geared towards the reader. The writer, in essence, is now working to help the reader develop knowledge on the topic. The three stages of this process are called knowledge telling, knowledge transforming and, knowledge crafting.[173]

I am hardly making the claim that I am an expert in any topic, or, that I am a great writer for that matter. Rather, I relate to this process because I have spent the better part of the past eleven years refining the way I write. When I first started there was an alarmist type of tone to my argument. I was trying to motivate people to act, but it was done in a way that probably made me look a little conspiratorial, if you will.

As the years went by, and I became more competent, I found I really enjoy writing research papers. So, I gradually shifted my style. I now approach everything from the perspective that I am providing information to the reader that they are probably unaware of, so I want it to appear professional. I understand that some of the information I am providing is a little unsettling and that people may be skeptical; therefore, I stick to credible sources. Most of what I claimed in this book is found in science journals or college textbooks. Being in a college textbook, given the liberal bias most of them hold, does not automatically equate with credibility. It does, however, show the mindset and beliefs of the far left.

People who take the time to read political books are looking for answers. What good does it do to describe the problem and not offer solutions? There is not a single solution to the problem we face. Not without a thorough understanding of how we got here. Writing and researching have been my solution. It is my contribution to the fight for liberty because I believe we all need to educate ourselves. It is me dedicating a part of myself to a larger purpose. The beautiful thing about America is we are a nation of individuals who all have unique abilities. If we are to preserve liberty for future generations, we must first commit to sticking to principle and holding people accountable. Even if it is a popular president.

The larger point is that I believe we all need to be the change we want to see. It is not enough to rally around a president and put all our hopes into empty promises and campaign slogans. That is what we have been doing, and it has gotten us nowhere. Millions of people loved President Trump, but for all his promises, he ended up being drowned by the swamp creatures he was supposed to drain. We must break away from this absolute loyalty to parties and partisan politics. The Democrat party is more united than ever while the Republican base, barely even exists anymore. A funny meme appeared on Facebook the other day. Some people will be angered by it, but I found it rather humorous because it portrayed an uncomfortable truth. It was a picture of Donald Trump smiling with a caption that alluded to the idea that he was a lifelong Democrat who handed the left the Presidency and both chambers of congress while simultaneously convincing millions he was the best conservative ever.

Donald Trump donated huge sums of money to the same politicians that acted as if they hated him. This was a fact that people never questioned. Another interesting correlation is that Trump and the Clinton's have a long history of friendship. One of the things that always bothered me was the fact that Hillary Clinton wrote her college thesis on Saul Alinsky and how to change government from within. It is titled *There is only the fight.* This alludes to the Alinsky mentality that the only thing that matters is the revolution.

One thing that I did not go into was the Qanon phenomenon. I wanted to stay away from sounding too conspiratorial. Q, as he had come to be known, was instrumental in shaping popular thought concerning Trump and his alleged plan to drain the swamp. Q was partially responsible for the creation of the four-dimensional chess game Trump voters believed he was playing. Throughout the duration of Trump's presidency, Q was communicating messages to his followers that led them to believe there was a grand plan to arrest the deep state and hold military tribunals for the guilty. It was like a dangling carrot being hung on a treadmill because Trump followers were chasing Q's theories, which were going nowhere.

Trump's voters put so much faith in Q they were still expecting these arrests to take place right up to January 6. The day congress certified the electoral votes for Joe Biden. It is hardly their fault. If any of the theories presented in this book are true, it is reasonable to assume that Q was a carefully orchestrated psychological warfare operation, taking advantage of people's fears, anxieties, hopes and beliefs. Which is exactly what propaganda is designed to do. The book *New Lies for Old*,[174] by Soviet defector Anatoliy Golitsyn, describes something similar called Operation Trust. This was an operation designed to get the Russian people to believe that the Communist revolutionaries would fail in their efforts and be arrested.

The controversy of the 2020 presidential election culminated with what was described as an angry mob of Trump supporters storming the capital building on January 6. There is reason to believe this was an orchestrated attempt to discredit his voters as violent radicals. Groups like Antifa are well known for posing as conservatives and committing acts of violence. For example, the organizer of the Unite the Right rally, where Trump supporters were portrayed as white supremacists, was organized by Josh Kessler who was an Occupy Wall Street organizer and an Obama supporter. This goes back to an Alinsky tactic where he told a group of college students in the early 70's to show up to George Bush speeches dressed as Klan members, and loudly cheer for everything he said.

There is no doubt that this so-called raid on the capital will be used as a pretext to push civilian disarmament and further discredit conservative ideals. At the time of this writing, we were four days away from Joe Biden's inauguration. There is no doubt that we have a massive challenge in front of us.

Again, this book is hardly complete, but I do believe it will lay the groundwork for developing a good understanding of how we got to this point. People are in a state of mindless compliance, following government dictates for reasons they cannot explain. The beliefs of the social scientists and the models they use to predict and control our behavior were described, as were the words of people who think we are too lazy to research for ourselves. If there is anything that can be taken from this book, understand that. They think we are too lazy and stupid to understand anything. If we are not paying attention or asserting the right to stand for our liberty, they will continue to hold this view.

About the Author

David Risselada is a graduate of Liberty University's Master of Professional Writing Program and holds a bachelor's degree in Social Work. David has been writing on the socio/political issues our nation faces since being exposed to the leftist agenda in social work education. David has two previous books: *Not on My Watch: Exposing the Marxist Agenda in Education* and *Psychopolitics in America: A Nation Under Conquest*. David's writing can be seen on his website, defenseofournation.com. He is also a regular contributor to Sons of Liberty Media. David served in the Marine Corps from 1995 to 1999 and the U.S. Army from 2001 to 2006. David lives with his wife of twenty-five years, Deborah, and has two daughters.

References

[1] The National Association of Scholars. The Scandal of Social Work Education Microsoft Word - scandal_of_soc_work_10sep07.doc (nas.org)

[2] Skousen, C. W. The Naked Communist (1958) The English Publishing Company. The Naked Communist: W. Cleon Skousen: Free Download, Borrow, and Streaming: Internet Archive

[3] Knoller, M. (2008, September 29) *Bush administrations adds $4 trillion to the national debt.* CBSNews.com

[4] Knoller, M. (2012, March 12) *National debt has increased more under Obama than under Bush.* CBSNews.com

[5] Healey, G. (2016, May 5) *President Obama's legacy is endless war.* Time.com

[6] http://www.visibility911.org/wp-content/uploads/2008/02/rebuildingamericasdefenses.pdf

[7] https://www.youtube.com/watch?v=9RC1Mepk_Sw&t=22s

[8] Liptak, K. (2014, September 23) *Countries bombed by the U.S. under the Obama administration.* CNN.com

[9] N.A. (2015, June 22) *15 Ways Bill Clinton's White House failed America and the world.* Alternet.com

[10] Newman, C. (2014, March 20) *The powerplay to eliminate the petrodollar.* Dailyreckoning.com

[11] Larison, D. (2020, June 25) *Trump escalates killer drone war, and no one seems to care.* TheAmericanconservative.com

[12] Rodriguez, E. (2020, May 14) *National debt has increased $5.2 trillion during Trump's 3 years as president.* Newsweek.com

[13] Quigley, C. *Tragedy and Hope: A History of the world in our time.* (1966) New York. The Macmillan Company

[14] Landers, E. (2019, February 28) *Trump to lawmakers: 'Take the guns first, go through due process second.'* Cnn.com

[15] Sullum, J. (2019, March 28) *Donald Trump's Bump Stock ban turns peaceful gun owners into felons by fiat.* Reason.com

[16] Alinsky, S. *Rules for Radicals.* (1971) New York. Vintage books.

[17] Perloff, R, M. *The dynamics of persuasion: Communications and attitudes in the 21st century* (2017) New York. Routledge

[18] Perloff, R, M. *The dynamics of persuasion: Communications and attitudes in the 21ˢᵗ century* (2017) New York. Routledge

[19] Dolinski, D., Ciszek, M., Godlewski, K. & Zawadski, M. (2002) Fear-then-relief: Mindlessness and cognitive deficits. *European journal of social; psychology*, 32(4) pp. 435-447

[20] Perloff, R, M. *The dynamics of persuasion: Communications and attitudes in the 21ˢᵗ century* (2017) New York. Routledge

[21] Perloff, R, M. *The dynamics of persuasion: Communications and attitudes in the 21ˢᵗ century* (2017) New York. Routledge

[22] Willer, R., & Feinberg, M. (2015, November 17) *The Key to Political Persuasion* The New York Times (Sunday Review)

[23] Nelson, T, E., Zoe, O, M. & Rosalee, C, A. (1997) Toward a psychology of framing effects. *Political behavior*, 19(3) pp. 221-246

[24] Hayes, D. (2016, June 14) I am an AR-15 owner and I have had enough. Thoughtcatalog.com

[25] Laboeuf, A, R. & Sharif, E. (2003) Deep thoughts and shallow frames: On the susceptibility of framing effects. *Journal of behavioral decision making*, 16. Pp. 77-92

26 Sunstein, C. & Thaler, R. *Nudge: Improving decisions about health, wealth, and happiness.* (2008) Yale University Press. New Haven & London.

27 Perloff, R, M. *The dynamics of persuasion: Communications and attitudes in the 21ˢᵗ century* (2017) New York. Routledge

28 Perloff, R, M. *The dynamics of persuasion: Communications and attitudes in the 21ˢᵗ century* (2017) New York. Routledge

29 Nunes, R. Dialectical Materialism (https://www.marxists.org/history/erol/new-zealand/nunes-marx-mao/nunes-dialectical.pdf)

30 Nightingale, Y.C. (2016, May 25) What is the Hegelian dialectic? https://christianobserver.net/what-is-the-hegelian-dialectic/

31 Burke, H. (2016, March 10) Federal money and federal control of schools. https://www.educationviews.org/federal-money-federal-control-schools/

32 Newman, A. (2013, August 8) Common core: A scheme to rewrite education. https://thenewamerican.com/common-core-a-scheme-to-rewrite-education/

33 Burke, H. (2016, March 10) Federal money and federal control of schools.
https://www.educationviews.org/federal-money-federal-control-schools/

34 Burke, H (2015, October 6) Common core college and career standards: Big fraud.

35 Cicotta, T. (2020, November 16) California school district bans 'To Kill a Mockingbird,' Huckleberry Finn' other classic novels. Breitbart

36 Lee, J., & Wu, Y. (2017). Is the Common Core racing America to the top? Tracking changes in state standards, school practices, and student achievement. Education Policy Analysis Archives, 25(35).
http://dx.doi.org/10.14507/epaa.25.2834

37 Rebarber, T. (2020) The common core debacle: Results from 2019 NAEP and other sources. *Pioneer Institute.* 205 https://files.eric.ed.gov/fulltext/ED604651.pdf

38 Kaye, K. (2020, February 27) *National Education Association pushes transgendered education in elementary schools.* https://legalinsurrection.com/2020/02/national-education-association-pushes-transgendered-education-in-elementary-schools/

39 Sheldon, L. (2001) Homosexuals recruit public school children. *Traditional values* 18 (11) 1-8

[40] Baker, G. (2020, May 8) How the 1619 project slandered America. The New York Post. https://nypost.com/2020/05/08/how-the-1619-project-slandered-america/

[41] Moore, M. (2020, September 23) Trump expands ban on critical race theory to federal contractors. The New York Post. https://nypost.com/2020/09/23/trump-expands-ban-on-critical-race-theory-to-federal-contractors/

[42] Nelson, S. (2020, November 2) Trump signs order to promote patriotic education on eve of election. The New York Post. https://nypost.com/2020/11/02/trump-signs-order-to-push-patriotic-education-on-eve-of-election/

[43] Berry, S. (2018, September 18) Devos signs onto globalist U.N. education agenda, grassroots parents call for her dismissal. Breitbart https://www.breitbart.com/politics/2018/09/18/devos-signs-onto-globalist-u-n-education-agenda-grassroots-parents-call-for-her-dismissal/

[44] Gutierrez, R. (2013) The sociopolitical turn in mathematics education. *Journal for research in mathematics education*, 44(1) pp. 37-68 retrieved from Google Scholar

[45] Kelner, D. (1990) Critical theory and the crisis of social theory. *Sociological perspectives,* 33(1) pp. 11-33. Retrieved from Goggle Scholar

[46] Bohman, J. (2005) Critical Theory. Stanford Encyclopedia of Philosophy. https://plato.stanford.edu/entries/critical-theory/#Bib

[47] Golitsyn, A. *The Perestroika Deception.* (1984) Edward Harle Limited. London

[48] Iserbyt, C. (1989) Soviets in the classroom. Americas Latest education fad. Deliberate dumbing down.com

[49] 1985 general agreement.pdf (thetechnocratictyranny.com)

[50] Branden, N. "The Psychology of Pleasure." From *The Virtue of Selfishness: A New Concept of Egoism.* Ayn Rand (ed.). New York: Signet, 1964

[51] Becker, W. Thomas, D. R. & Carnine, D. (1969) Reducing behavior problems: An operant conditioning guide for teachers. Retrieved online

[52] Thomas, A (1927) From *The Deliberate Dumbing Down of America: A chronological paper trail, p.11. Ohio,* Conscience Press.

[53] Socialism: Fabian and Marxist Socialism. Socialism: Fabian and Marxist Socialism (politicalsciencenotes.com)

[54] Socialism: Fabian and Marxist Socialism. Socialism: Fabian and Marxist Socialism (politicalsciencenotes.com)

[55] *Dewey, J. Democracy and Education.* (1916) Northwood Mass. The Macmillan Company

[56] Skinner, B. F. *Science and human behavior* (1953) Pearson education.

[57] Becker, W., Thomas, D. R. & Carnine, D. (1969) Reducing behavior problems: An operant conditioning guide for teachers. Retrieved online

[58] Skinner, B, F. *Beyond freedom and dignity.* (1971) Middlesex England: Penguin books ltd

[59] Insko, C. (1965) Verbal reinforcement of attitude. Journal of personality and social psychology. 2(4) pp. 621-623

[60] Festinger, L., & Carlsmith, J. M. (1959). Cognitive consequences of forced compliance. *The Journal of Abnormal and Social Psychology, 58*(2), 203–210

[61] Festinger, L. *A theory of cognitive dissonance.* (1957) Palo Alto, CA: Stanford University Press

[62] Child drugging: Psychiatry destroying lives. Report and recommendations on fraudulent psychiatric diagnoses and the enforced drugging of youth. (2008) *Citizens Commission on Human Rights.*

[63] Ritalin Side Effects. (N.K.D.) *Citizens Commission on Human Rights*

[64] Saul, R. (2014, March 14) *Doctor: ADHD does not exist.* Time Magazine. Retrieved from https://time.com/25370/doctor-adhd-does-not-exist/

[65] DSM Criteria for ADHD: The ADD Resource Center. Retrieved from https://www.addrc.org/dsm-5-criteria-for-adhd

[66] ADHD is a Fraud. (2018, December 2015) Citizens Commission on Human Rights St. Louis. Retrieved from http://www.cchrstl.org/wordpress/2018/12/15/adhd-is-a-fraud

[67] Whitaker, R. (2005) Anatomy of an epidemic: Psychiatric drugs and the astonishing rise of mental illness in America. Ethical human psychology and psychiatry. (7) 1 p. 25.

[68] Hymen, S, E. & Nester, E, J. (1996) Initiation and action: A paradigm for understanding psychotropic drug action. *American journal of psychiatry.* (153) 2 p. 161.

[69] ADHD Tests Webmd ADHD/ADD Tests for Diagnosis: Medical Testing, Scales, & Psychological Criteria (webmd.com)

[70] ADHD in Children: When a teacher recognizes ADHD symptoms. Webmd A Teacher's Role in Diagnosing Child ADHD in the Classroom (webmd.com)

[71] Miller, C. (2019) Are schools driving ADHD diagnoses? The Child Mind Institute.

[72] Lo, B. & Grady, D. (2017) Payments to physicians: Does the amount of money make a difference? *Journal American medical association,* 317(17) 1719-1720.

[73] Cosgrove, L., Krimsky, S., Vijayaraghavan, M., & Schneider, L. (2006) Financial ties between DSM-IV panel members and the pharmaceutical industry. *Psychotherapy and psychosomatics. (75)* 154-160

[74] Inventing disorders: For drug profit. Citizens commission on human rights Official Report: Inventing Disorders for Drug Profits (cchr.org)

[75] Rhodewalt, F. & Comer, R. (1979) Induced compliance attitude change. *Journal of experimental social psychology* 15(1) pp. 35-47

[76] Martin, Y, P., Hamilton, E, V., Mckimmie, M, B., Terry, J, D. & Martin, R. (2006) Effects of caffeine on persuasion and attitude change: The role of secondary tasks in manipulating systematic message processing. *European journal of social psychology,* 37(2) pp. 320-338

[77] Breggin, Peter R. (2000). What psychologists and therapists need to know about ADHD and stimulants. *CHANGES-SHEFFIELD*, 18(1), 13–23.

[78] Breggin, Peter R. (2000). What psychologists and therapists need to know about ADHD and stimulants. *CHANGES-SHEFFIELD*, 18(1), 13–23.

[79] Perring, C. (1997) Medicating children: The case for Ritalin. *Bioethics*, 11(3&4) pp. 228-240

[80] Perring, C. (1997) Medicating children: The case for Ritalin. *Bioethics*, 11(3&4) pp. 228-240

[81] Harming Youth: Screening and Drugs Ruin Young Minds Official Report on Harming Youth (cchr.org)

[82] Ruffalo, M. (2017, November 1) Tranquilizing humanity into oblivion. Psychology Today

[83] Total Number of People Taking Psychiatric Drugs in the United States | CCHR International

[84] Ventegodt, S., Andersen, J, N.& Kandel, I. (2009) An Ethical Analysis of Contemporary Use of Coercive Persuasion (Brainwashing and Mind Control) in Psychiatry. *Journal of alternative medicine research,* 1(2) pp. 177-188.

[85] Szasz, T. (1960) The myth of mental illness. *American psychologist*, 15. Pp. 113-118.

[86] Ventegodt, S., Andersen, J, N.& Kandel, I. (2009) An Ethical Analysis of Contemporary Use of Coercive Persuasion (Brainwashing and Mind Control) in

Psychiatry. *Journal of alternative medicine research,* 1(2) pp. 177-188.

[87] Franzini, R, L. & McDonald, D, R. (1973) Marijuana use and hypnotic susceptibility. Journal of consulting and clinical psychology, 40(2) pp. 176-180

[88] Skinner, B, F. *Beyond freedom and dignity.* Middlesex England: Penguin books ltd. 1971

[89] Rachels, J. *Created from animals: The moral implications of Darwinism.* Oxford University Press. 1990. 129-173

[90] Jost, T, J. Glaser, J., Kruglanski, W, A. & Sulloway, J, F. (2003) Political conservatism as motivated social cognition. *Psychological bulletin,* 129(3) pp. 339-375.

[91] Courtois, S., Werth, N., Panne, L, J., Paczkowski, A., Bartosek, K. & Margolin, L, S. *The Black Book of Communism* (1999) Harvard University Press. Cambridge Ma.

[92] Perloff, J. *Tornado in a junkyard.* (1999) Refuge books, Arlington

[93] Barzun, J. *Darwin, Marx, Wagner: Critique of a heritage, 2ⁿᵈ ed.* (1958) Double day, Garden City NY.

[94] Skinner, B, F. *Beyond freedom and dignity.* Middlesex England: Penguin books ltd. 1971

95 Perloff, R, M. *The dynamics of persuasion: Communications and attitudes in the 21ˢᵗ century* (2017) New York. Routledge

96 Cantril, H. *The Invasion Form Mars: A Study in the Psychology of Panic* (1940) Princeton university Press, Princeton N.J.

97 Wallis, C. (2018, January 9) The New Science of Happiness. *Time Magazine.* Content.time.com

98 Todhunter, C. (2020, November 9) *Dystopian "Great Reset:" "Own Nothing and be Happy, Being Human in 2030.* Global Research - Centre for Research on Globalization

99 TRANSFORMING OUR WORLD: THE 2030 AGENDA FOR SUSTAINABLE DEVELOPMENT. Retrieved from 21252030 Agenda for Sustainable Development web.pdf (un.org)

100 Wu, J. (2019, January 10) *Capitalism is Dangerous for Your Mental Health.* Reason in Revolt

101 Lewis, C. S. (1987) "The Humanitarian Theory of Punishment," *Issues in Religion and Psychotherapy*: 13 (1), pp. 224-230. imageREAL Capture (austlii.edu.au)

102 Sunstein, C. & Thaler, R. *Nudge: Improving decisions about health, wealth, and happiness.* (2008) Yale University Press. New Haven & London.

[103] Davidai, S., Gilouich, T., Ross, D. T. (2012) The meaning of default options for potential organ donors. *PNAS* 109(38)

[104] Mello, M. M., Silverman, J. D. & Saad, O. B. (2020) Ensuring uptake of vaccines against sars-vov-2. *The New England journal of medicine,* 383(14) pp.1-4

[105] McGregor, J. (2020, December 2) *Employers prepare for coronavirus vaccine with a question: Can we require it?* The Washington Post.

[106] Executive Order -- Using Behavioral Science Insights to Better Serve the American People | whitehouse.gov (archives.gov)

[107] Cantril, H. *The Invasion Form Mars: A Study in the Psychology of Panic* (1940) Princeton university Press, Princeton N.J.

[108] Ansary, A. (2005, December 29) Mass mind control through network television: Are your thoughts your own? *Rense.com*

[109] Cantril, H. & Strunk, M. *Public Opinion 1935-1946.* (1951) Princeton University Press, Princeton New Jersey.

[110] Ansary, A. (2005, December 29) Mass mind control through network television: Are your thought your own? *Rense.com*

[111] <u>Rand Corporation - Media Bias Fact Check</u>

[112] Folkenflik, D. (2020, November 7) *With Trump's loss, Murdoch's Fox News faces wrath and tough choices.* www.NPR.org

[113] Reynolds, E. (2020, July 17) *Fox News family's James Murdoch and wife donate 1.2 million to Joe Biden.* The Federalist.com

[114] Harris, N. (2020, December 4) *Fox News' Murdoch's loved Clinton crime foundation, crooked Hillary.* Newspunch.com

[115] Hanchett, I. (2017, February 22) Brzezinski: *Controlling what people think is our job.* Breitbart.com

[116] Herman, S. & Chomsky, N. *The manufacturing of consent: The political economy of the mass media.* (1988) Pantheon books, New York.

[117] Herman, S. & Chomsky, N. *The manufacturing of consent: The political economy of the mass media.* (1988) Pantheon books, New York.

[118] Louise, M. (2016, October 10) *Operation Mockingbird: CIA Media Manipulation.* Targetedjustice.net

[119] Constantine, A. (1996) *The tainted legacy of operation mockingbird.* <u>The Tainted Legacy of Operation</u>

<u>MOCKINGBIRD</u> – Alex Constantine – 1996 – Church of Mabus Radio

[120] An apocalyptic synthesis. <u>www.amallulla.org</u>

[121] Bois, P. (2020, December 17) *Dr. Fauci: American independent spirit made pandemic worse.* ClarionNews.com

[122] Zhou, L. (2020, December 17) *Poll: Americans care a lot more about covid 19 relief than the national debt right now. "Americans prioritize economic relief over reigning in debt."* Vox.com

[123] H.R.6496 - 116th Congress (2019-2020): Emergency Money for the People Act | Congress.gov | Library of Congress

[124] Tillison, T. (2020, December 23) *Trump calls for revamp of 'disgrace' relief bill, almost nothing to do with covid, Dems only jump on 2K bump.* Bizpacreview.com

[125] Gittleson, B. (2020, March 16) *White House issues new guidelines for stopping spread of Coronavirus. Trump explains everyone needed to comply for them to slow the spread.* ABC News.

[126] Gonzalez, O. (2020, April 15) *Trump halts WHO funding. Bill Gates, others say that's a mistake.* Cnet.com

[127] Walia, A. (2020, July 29) *Trump gives 1.6 billion to Bill Gates' vaccine alliance, inks deal with Pfizer for vaccine.* Collectiveevolution.com, retrieved from Lewrockwell.com

128 Merica, D. & Liptak, K. (2020, March 26) *The history of Trump and Cuomo's hot and cold relationship.* CNN.com

129 Castronuovo, C. (2020, November 11) *Trump battles Cuomo over vaccine plan.* MSN.com

130 Gander, K. (2020, December 22) *Anthony Fauci says new covid strain in U.K. has probably reached the U.S.* Newsweek

131 Streb, M., Conway, M, A. & Michael, T. (2017) Conditioned responses to trauma reminders: How durable are they overtime and does memory integration reduce them? *Journal of behavior therapy and experimental psychology,* (57) pp. 1-26.

132 Mandelbaum, E. (2015) Associationists theory of thought. *The Stanford encyclopedia of philosophy*

133 Tunnenbaum, M, M., Helpe, J., Zimmerman, R, S., Saul, L., Jacobs, S., Wilson, K. & Albarracin, D. (2015) Appealing to fear: A meta-analysis of fear appeal effectiveness and theories. *Psychological bulletin* 141(6) pp. 1178-1204

134 Perloff, R, M. *The dynamics of persuasion: Communications and attitudes in the 21ˢᵗ century* (2017) New York. Routledge

[135]Dolinski, D., Ciszek, M., Godlewski, K. & Zawadski, M. (2002) Fear-then-relief: Mindlessness and cognitive deficits. *European journal of social; psychology*, 32(4) pp. 435-447

[136] Tunnenbaum, M, M., Helpe, J., Zimmerman, R, S., Saul, L., Jacobs, S., Wilson, K. & Albarracin, D. (2015) Appealing to fear: A meta-analysis of fear appeal effectiveness and theories. *Psychological bulletin* 141(6) pp. 1178-1204

[137] Tunnenbaum, M, M., Helpe, J., Zimmerman, R, S., Saul, L., Jacobs, S., Wilson, K. & Albarracin, D. (2015) Appealing to fear: A meta-analysis of fear appeal effectiveness and theories. *Psychological bulletin* 141(6) pp. 1178-1204

[138] Williams, K, C. (2012) Fear appeal theory. *International journal of economics and business research*. (5) pp. 63-82

[139]Perloff, R, M. *The dynamics of persuasion: Communications and attitudes in the 21ˢᵗ century* (2017) New York. Routledge

[140] Williams, K, C. (2012) Fear appeal theory. *International journal of economics and business research*. (5) pp. 63-82

[141] Williams, K, C. (2012) Fear appeal theory. *International journal of economics and business research.* (5) pp. 63-82

[142] Williams, K, C. (2012) Fear appeal theory. *International journal of economics and business research.* (5) pp. 63-82

[143] Simpson, K, J. (2017) Appeal to fear in health care: Appropriate or inappropriate? *Chiropractic and manual therapies.* (25)27, pp. 1-10

[144] Raamkumar, A., Tan, G, S. & Wee, L, H. (2020) Use of the health belief model-Based deep learning classifiers for covid-19 social media content to examine public perceptions of physical distancing: model development and case study. *JMIR Public health and surveillance.* 6(3)

[145] Champion, L, V. & Skinner, S, C. (2008) The health belief model. From *Health behavior and health education.* (2008) Edited by Glanz, K., Rimer, B, K. & Viswanath, K. Jossey Bass. San Francisco, Ca.

[146] Champion, L, V. & Skinner, S, C. (2008) The health belief model. From *Health behavior and health education.* (2008) Edited by Glanz, K., Rimer, B, K. & Viswanath, K. Jossey Bass. San Francisco, Ca.

[147] Simpson, K, J. (2017) Appeal to fear in health care: Appropriate or inappropriate? *Chiropractic and manual therapies.* (25)27, pp. 1-10

[148] COVID-19 Pandemic Planning Scenarios | CDC

[149] Fauci, A, S., Lane, C. & Redfield, R. R. (2020) Covid-19: Navigating the uncharted. *The New England Journal of Medicine.* 382, pp. 1268-1269

[150] Saxena, V. (2020, August 2) *CDC admits hospitals, medical folks have 'perverse incentive' to falsely count covid deaths.* Bizpacreview.com

[151] Bondy, D. (2020, September 1) *CDC: 94% of Covid-19 deaths had underlying medical conditions.* MSN.com

[152] Sunstein, C. & Thaler, R. *Nudge: Improving decisions about health, wealth, and happiness.* (2008) Yale University Press. New Haven & London.

[153] Provisional Death Counts for Coronavirus Disease 2019 (COVID-19) (cdc.gov)

[154] N.K A. (2020, December 21) *PCR tests create false positives: Is there a hidden agenda?* Mercola.com

[155] CDC 2019-Nover Coronavirus (2019-nCOV) Real time RT-PCR diagnostic panel. Center for disease control and prevention.

156 Corbett, K, P. (2020) Where is the evidence for the existence of the 'novel coronavirus,' 'Sars-Cov-2'? evidencenotfear.com

157 Sim, S, W., Moey Peter, S. K. & Tan, N, C. (2014) The use of facemasks to prevent respiratory infection: A literature review in the context of the health belief model. *Singapore medical journal.* 55(3) pp. 160-167

158 Bundgaard, H. & Bundgaard, J, S. (2020) Effectiveness of adding a mask recommendation to other public health measures to prevent sars-cov-2 in Danish mask wearers. *Annals of internal medicine.* (acpjournals.org)

159 Macintyre, C, R. & Chughtai, A, A. (2020) A rapid systematic review of the efficacy of facemasks and respirators against coronaviruses and other respiratory transmissible viruses for the community, healthcare workers and sick patients. *National Library of Medicine* PubMed (nih.gov)

160 Feuer, W. & Higgins-Dunn, N. (2020, June 8) *Asymptomatic spread of coronavirus is 'very rare,' WHO says.* CNBC.com

161 Fox, M. (2020, November 20) *Most coronavirus cases are spread by people without symptoms, CDC now says.* CNN.com

[162] Shiyi, C., Yong, G., Wang, C., Bachmann, M., Shanbo, W., Jie, G., Yuchai, H., Wang, T., Li, L., Lu, K., Jiang, H., Yanhong, G., Xu, H., Shen, X., Qingfeng, T., Chuanzhu, L., Fujian, S., Xiaoxv, Y., & Zuxun, L. (2020). Post-lockdown SARS-CoV-2 nucleic acid screening in nearly ten million residents of Wuhan, China. *Nature Communications, 11*(1)

[163] The Health Belief Model (bu.edu)

[164] The Health Belief Model (bu.edu)

[165] Skinner, B, F. *Beyond freedom and dignity.* (1971) Middlesex England: Penguin books ltd.

[166] Maich, G, H, K. (2013) Reducing Cognitive Dissonance Through Effort Justification: Evidence from Past Studies and Daily Experience. *WUPJ* (1)

[167] Mcclay, B. D. (2018). Virtue Signaling. *Hedgehog Review, 20*(2), 141–143.

[168] Groves, H. (2020, April 29) The psychological manipulation of universal masking. *Health Freedom Ohio.*

[169] Raamkumar, A., Tan, G, S. & Wee, L, H. (2020) Use of the Health Belief Model-based deep learning classifiers for Covid-19 social media content to examine public perceptions of physical distancing: Model development and case study. *JMIR Public health and surveillance.* 6(3)

[170] Andrews, A. *How do you kill 11 million people? Why the truth matters more than you think.* (2011) Nashville, Tennessee. W publishing.

[171] Schumm, L. (2014, June 2) What was Operation Paperclip? *History.com*

[172] Brainwashing: A Synthesis on the Russian Textbook of psychopolitics. Healing unlimited Christianscience.org Brain-Washing (Mind-Changing) - Part 1 of 3 (israelect.com)

[173] Kellogg, R, T. (2008) Training writing skills: A cognitive development perspective. *Journal of writing research.* 1(1) pp. 1-26

[174] Golitsyn, A. New Lies for Old: The communist strategy of deception and misinformation. (1984) GSG & Associates Retrieved from <u>New lies for old ones: Golitsyn: Free Download, Borrow, and Streaming: Internet Archive</u>

www.ingramcontent.com/pod-product-compliance
Lightning Source LLC
Chambersburg PA
CBHW070120260726

48658CB00001B/183